It's Your Business

It's Your Business

BY JOHN HARRIMAN

Houghton Mifflin Company : Boston
The Riverside Press : Cambridge

1 9 6 0

For Jane and Gay

LIBRARY OF CONGRESS CATALOG CARD NUMBER: 60-9392

FIRST PRINTING

PRINTED IN THE U.S.A.

Preface

THIS is a journalist's book, not an economic analysis. It was written while the issues with which it deals were unfolding, and with the hope of reaching as wide an audience as possible with what I believe to be the great underlying story of our times.

For these reasons I have tried to simplify somewhat one or two of the more complicated problems facing us today in economic policy. I do not think I have distorted these, however, nor in any way shaped them to define a thesis or to support conclusions.

Businessmen in Europe are much less accessible to newspapermen than in the United States, and I want to thank those in this country who opened for me so many doors on the Continent: Philip J. Potter and Louis C. Farley, Jr., of the State Street Bank and Trust Company of Boston, sponsors of my radio program — the former for valuable contacts in the German Ruhr and West Berlin, the latter for those remarkable letters which gave me access to bank economists over most of Europe; and Baron Charles de Pampelonne, Consul General of France in Boston, who put me in touch with the Patronat Français and France Actuelle in Paris, where Bertrand Hommey, Stephen Laird and Anne de Nanteuil aided me so much with material, advice and introductions.

In Italy, I was guided through the intricacies of the industrial scene by Stanley Hillyer of Hillyer Associates, management and engineering consultants of Milan, and by the wisdom of Carlo Calosi, vice-president for Europe of the Raytheon Company.

Finally I must express my gratitude to two old friends and associates, Laurence L. Winship and Victor O. Jones, editor and managing editor of the *Boston Globe,* who saw the story emerging in Europe as early as 1957 and sent me to Europe twice to report on it.

JOHN HARRIMAN

Cambridge, Massachusetts
1960

Contents

I	"You Are Talking to a Bear"	1
II	Threat and Opportunity — Overseas	6
III	The Story of Aluminum	11
IV	Rebuilt Europe — Competitor and Ally	17
V	The Rebuilding of Japan	25
VI	Competition Begins to Hurt	31
VII	Typewriters, Tape, and the Treaty of Rome	37
VIII	Investment in Europe Becomes a Trek	45
IX	The European Challenge, More Than Price	54
X	1957-59 — The "Gold Years"	59
XI	The Lesson of Hard Money	68
XII	Stabilization in Britain and Germany	74
XIII	The "Hard" Franc Ushers in a New Decade	81
XIV	Transistors and Textiles from Across the Pacific	95
XV	The "Voluntary" Quota	102

XVI   *"Creeping" Protectionism*   110

XVII   *Europe at "Sixes and Sevens"*   116

XVIII   *Four Wise Men*   123

XIX   *A New Soviet Voice?*   131

XX   *Trade Wars Are for Keeps*   139

XXI   *The World Companies*   146

XXII   *When Will Labor Speak?*   153

XXIII   *A North Atlantic Economic Community?*   161

XXIV   *What the U. S. Has to Fear*   167

XXV   *Unity or Bravo?*   177

It's Your Business

I

"You Are Talking to a Bear"

ON THE AFTERNOON of January 21, 1960, newspaper correspondents reported from London that the British bank rate that day had been raised from 4 per cent to 5 per cent.

It is hard to think of an event less apt to arouse the interest of the American commuter, homeward bound to his suburban ranch house, than that a few banks halfway across the world would in the future have to pay more for their discounts, or borrowings, at the Bank of England. And the story was hardly mentioned in the evening press. Besides, there was so much of more immediate and personal interest in the newspapers that day. The Finch murder case was going full blast out in Los Angeles, with an admitted hired killer denying that he had been retained to seduce, rather than kill, Barbara Finch. Moscow that day announced its latest missile launching over the Pacific. And Washington expressed the hope that any disarmament talks could include the Red Chinese.

As for the economic news, the stock market was continuing a decline that was rubbing the bloom off recent speculative commitments, worry enough for the twelve million stock-owning Americans. And if it was money rates you were going to talk about . . . newspapers that same afternoon

reported that the building industry was concerned that high
mortgage rates might mean fewer American homes built in
the current year.

Furthermore, the dispatch from London was itself disarm-
ing. It stated that the reason for the rise in the British bank
rate was the fear of "inflationary factors" appearing in the
British economy — in short, that the British were simply
doing what our own Federal Reserve had been doing: tightening the screws a little in monetary policy to prevent a boom
with inflationary overtones from getting out of hand.

Yet that rise in the British rate marked a turning point in
the economic history of our times. It brought an era to its
final closing — although the curtain had started down a full
two years before. It meant that American industry and
American labor faced new realities, that American workers
as well as management were to be forced to new responsibili-
ties, and that in economic policy we probably could never
again act with the complete freedom possible to us in the
past.

The first understanding of what the event in London
meant appeared on January 22 in the financial press. It was
pointed out that morning that if the purpose was, as stated,
simply to hold down on inflationary tendencies, the rise in
the British rate would have been on the order of ¼ of 1 per
cent, or at the most ½ of 1 per cent . . . not the full 1 per
cent.

By the following day it was also generally understood in
international financial circles that the sterling area was to
show a loss of gold and convertible currencies in January —
the fourth consecutive month of loss — and that the final
figures, January to January, would show a loss of some $450
million for the year.

This put a new complexion on the move in London, and
raised doubts about statements by the British authorities
that the Bank of England had been acting largely out of

concern with inflationary strains in the domestic economy. Within a few days, financial circles in New York were convinced that the real reason for the British move was to protect the pound against a drift of funds out of London to West Germany and the United States.

As a matter of fact, the brilliant economic writer Edgar L. Dale, Jr., of the *New York Times,* had seen this instantly. To his newspaper's London dispatch reporting the action of the Bank of England on January 22, Dale had added a story from Washington in which he stated that "the increase [in the bank rate] sent a shiver resembling fear through some circles of the economic community here today."

This fear, Dale reported, was that the deficit in the balance of payments of the United States had put the United States in the same position as Britain — that is, a position in which monetary policy must be strongly influenced by international conditions. In short, that we could no longer act unilaterally, considering only our domestic economy. This raised the possibility, Dale pointed out, that in the event of another recession in this country cheap money, a classic antirecession weapon, might be denied to the Federal Reserve.

Another way of saying this was that just as Britain had had to raise interest rates to protect the pound, so might we someday be unable to lower interest rates without exposing the dollar to dangerous pressure. Some opinion went even further. Within twenty-four hours of the London move, it was being predicted in informed circles here that the United States would have to counter the British move by lowering our own Federal Reserve rediscount rates . . . probably after the next U. S. Treasury financing. That in effect we were going to have to counter Britain's move to protect the pound by a similar move on our part to protect the dollar.

Nine days later, the magazine *Business Week,* a publication certainly not given to exaggeration or sensationalism, editorialized on the situation under the head: "The Fight for Gold Reserves." Said the editorial in part: "The Western capitals are being driven to jack up interest rates competitively." And in the same issue the magazine carried an article with the title: "Worldwide Interest Rate War?"

That such a war existed or was in the offing was of course denied immediately in London, Bonn and New York. This was to be expected. In the reserved, cautious, sensation-hating world of central banking the expression "interest rate war" must have seemed like very nasty words. But others had fewer compunctions.

A writer on finance and economics meets all kinds, the giants and the pygmies, the brilliant and the obtuse, the pretentious and the wise.

But there is in a small guarded office in Boston a certain man. This man was once managing director of a large private banking firm in Europe. He made a fortune in the American stock market in the 1920's, sold out in 1928, and between 1928 and 1938 operated almost exclusively in arbitrage — the buying and selling of money and securities in different countries for an immediate sale at a higher price.

In 1938, he went back into the security markets here in the United States, first in depressed railroad bonds, then in 1947 into stocks. He had unquestionably been one of the most successful operators in the market during the past decade, a man of profound economic insight.

On the day the news of the bank rate was flashed from London, the author of this book spoke to that man, asking if this might not at some future time mean an "interest rate war." The answer was immediate: "We already have it."

"And it means?"

"That economically we are no longer masters in our own house."

"And the future?"

The man smiled. "You are talking to a bear."

The events of this third week of January followed by only a month the usual optimistic forecasts for the new year — forecasts which, waxing quite eloquent, were stretched out to cover the coming decade.

Economists and business writers spoke of the "Golden Sixties," the promise of a new era of rapid growth sparked by science in which mankind was to penetrate the frontiers of space. The economic problems of this earth remained, of course, or at least some of them; but they would be melted by the heat of a new challenge, buried as man reached for the stars.

As for the past decade, it had been good, everyone agreed — more than good — the "Fabulous Fifties."

The 1950's had indeed been fabulous. They had been years of great prosperity and rapid economic growth, years in which the war-ravaged economies of Europe and Japan had been rebuilt, years in which economists of the West could come to the conclusion that never again were we likely to suffer the deep depressions of the past, years which opened new frontiers in technology and science.

But the same decade created a new world economy, to which the American people would have to adjust, a world economy in which our whole financial security and well-being was susceptible to changes brought about by a decision of a few men to change a central bank rate in distant London.

II

Threat and Opportunity
—Overseas

THE TREATY OF ROME was signed on March 25, 1957. Representatives of six nations put their names to that document — France, West Germany, Italy, Belgium, Holland and Luxembourg. Later the Treaty was ratified by each of those countries, and the European Economic Community came into being, the so-called European Common Market. This was the turning point. Here the American people entered a new era.

For a generation United States industry and labor had been dwelling on an economic Olympus. The economy of this country had stood alone, immeasurably stronger, more productive, more efficient than that of any other nation or group of nations. American goods and industrial techniques set the standards of the market place and were in demand throughout the world. The dollar ruled in financial centers, the equivalent of the gold for which the United States stood ready to pay $35 an ounce, a tower of strength among other currencies.

There had been, to be sure, an erosion of this sole economic supremacy going on for some time. The Soviet Union was rising from the rubble left by Hitler's defeated armies and building a modern economic state. We heard talk and read statistics — figures on Soviet steel and coal and oil, projections of an enormous burst in production which was to carry the Soviet growth trend upwards until at some future date Russian economic power and industrial output might be the equal of our own.

But we found this hard to believe. The U.S.S.R. was, after all, still a backward state, economically isolated and ruled by the remote, almost Oriental figure of Stalin, a nation of peasants which, while it might ape the methods of heavy industry of the West, could never play a really important role in the world economy.

It is easy to believe what one wants to believe, and we wanted to believe that capitalism was very efficient and communism very inefficient; and we told ourselves that the U.S.S.R. was and would remain a nation preoccupied with the problems of internal political and economic unrest and unable to exert power and influence outside its borders as long as we held preponderance in military power — at first through our having "the bomb," later through our own Strategic Air Command and the forces of the North Atlantic Treaty Organization.

The illusion of relative Soviet weakness we held quite firmly. Although somewhat shaken, it was not even destroyed by the first Soviet nuclear explosion. And even as it did finally begin to fade, we could still rationalize the reality which came thrusting itself before our eyes in the early 1950's by thinking of mounting Soviet economic strength as a "challenge" (a convenient but in this sense relatively meaningless term) . . . as the "cold war" (a contest which this country could not help but win in the long run because of our huge economic supremacy).

Besides, who could believe the statistics which the commissars put out? Who would credit their claims? No, the future would follow inevitably in the footsteps of the past. The dollar would remain impregnable, buttressed not only by the gold stored in our vaults, but by the vast industrial productiveness of our farmland, our assembly lines, and the rolling mills of Pittsburgh, East Chicago and Gary.

Then came the Treaty of Rome.

The effect of this treaty on American thinking was two-fold. For some time United States firms had been stepping up investment in Europe, but now this direct investment in plant abroad became, for many companies, a necessity; and the eyes with which American business had been watching the international scene were forced to a new focus. American business was being swept toward a new international outlook, in which it was no longer possible to dismiss the economic power of the Soviet Union.

The result of this was a change in treatment of Soviet economic news in the business press. Claims which had been reported with skepticism became the subject of alarmist articles. Groups such as the Russian Research Center at Harvard attained a sudden prominence. Teams of American industrial technicians visited the U.S.S.R., and returned with reports of rapid progress and impressive skills — that Russian oil drilling equipment was probably the best in the world, for instance, and that in some areas Russian steel production methods could match those of Pittsburgh. And a year later Allen W. Dulles, director of the Central Intelligence Agency, sent a shiver through the business community when he predicted that Russia was building economic power at such a rate that her output could equal that of this country shortly after 1970.

At the same time we realized that the new Europe which had been brought into being in part through our assistance with Marshall Plan aid was itself on the verge of an explosive growth, matching perhaps that of the Soviet Union and certainly exceeding that of the United States. More significantly, we saw in this Europe, both an opportunity and, possibly, a threat . . . an opportunity for American industry to share to its profit in this projected growth, and the threat of a dangerous competitor in both the world and our own domestic markets.

Internationalism was being brought home with a vengeance to the American business mind. And the fact that across the Atlantic, and spanning the Eurasian land mass, were rising two separate and distinct economies which together held both threat and promise for industry here sent large numbers of executives to the charts of their marketing experts and the drawing boards of their engineers.

There was between, let us say, 1956 and 1959, a profound revolution in business thinking in the United States. In these years, concepts long held were being re-examined, theories re-evaluated, and new plans being projected. Here was a historic turning point in the industrial history of the West.

It is interesting that the Treaty of Rome, and the European Common Market brought into existence by that Treaty, was the catalyst to this turning point. There were several reasons for this, but the primary one was probably the opportunity that the Common Market opened.

Business in the United States was used to the threat of foreign competition, and the dangers in the rise of Soviet economic power were only an extension or exaggeration of that threat. But that across the Atlantic lay a chance for expansion that would show up in fat figures on a corporate balance sheet was something new to American executives — or at least to a majority of them. The Common Market first touched American industry on the nerve of its profit motive, than which there is nothing more sensitive, more quick to react.

In dozens of industries management realized that their most important market was no longer the domestic market, and that by their success in the domestic market they could no longer measure their over-all achievement — in short, that the primary area in which to exercise their talents now lay overseas.

This awareness is yet to have its full impact. When it

does, it will change the policies of hundreds of corporations, and the lives of millions of workers, in such unrelated industries as the electronics firms of California and Massachusetts, the auto plants of Detroit, the textile mills of the Piedmont, and the complex of heavy industry along the southern shore of the Great Lakes, blacksmith shop to the economic power of the West.

A curtain is being run down on an economic era.

III

The Story of Aluminum

THE UNITED STATES . . . the Soviet Union . . . Europe
. . . Japan . . . these are the focal points of trade and economic power in the world today. The role of Japan will be
dealt with later. That country was not immediately affected
by the Rome Treaty, and it was this document which deline-
ated the new economic community of Europe and its interrelationship with the Soviet Union and the United States.

This interrelationship is complicated, varying from industry to industry, and further confused by its potential effect
on monetary policy, the balance of payments on foreign
account, and considerations of a purely political nature
where the Soviet Union is concerned. But it is possible to
get some understanding of it by taking just one industry,
aluminum, and examining developments in the postwar
years.

Here is an industry which at the close of World War II
might have been considered the particular field of Canada
and the United States.

The primary cost factor in aluminum production is electric power, and in the Pacific Northwest and the rushing
rivers of Canada is some of the cheapest hydroelectric power
on earth. Furthermore, the United States had plentiful sup-

plies of natural gas, also a cheap fuel when aluminum reduction plants can be set down adjacent to the wells. Finally, we led both in production techniques and in developing new markets for this metal of the future destined for widening use in many different lines, from building construction to "tin" cans.

Prior to World War II, the United States and Canada accounted for over a third of the world's production, and their metal sold far under the world price. In Europe, Germany was the most important producer, having built her industry during World War I on bauxite ore from Hungary. (Bauxite is the ore from which the metal is made.) To this step Germany was forced when cut off from most nonferrous metals by Allied blockade of the sea lanes.

But German aluminum was high-cost — the industry was state-owned and heavily subsidized — and it was not a factor in the world market, Germany being a net importer even then. France, the other significant producer at that time on the continent, had an output of only some 45,000 tons a year.

The first change in the picture in aluminum came at the close of World War II, when the Russians stripped the industries of East Germany, Hungary and Manchuria. Two years later Soviet output had soared, from 55,000 tons annually in 1939 to 99,000 in 1947.

In that year the Russians attempted to buy aluminum from this country and Canada, but were refused on the grounds that the metal was a strategic raw material used for armament. The Kremlin responded by building up its own production over the next few years to about 735,000 tons, using in large part the cheap hydroelectric power on the lower Volga.

By 1958 Russian capacity stood at 23 per cent of world capacity, and in that year the Soviet Union made its first major shift in its strategy in air power, from aircraft to missile.

This resulted in a surplus of aluminum, and the small amounts of the metal that Russia had been feeding into the world market were suddenly augmented. In just eighteen months the Russians flooded the British market with over 80,000 tons of metal at a considerable reduction from the world price.

This hit Canada's Aluminium Limited hard; and that company, after a rather frantic effort to sew up its British customers with what were called "loyalty contracts," replied on April 1, 1958, with a cut of two cents a pound. United States producers were forced to follow, and throughout the industry was a great wringing of hands.

One investment house in New York, in an appraisal of what it called the "opening gambit" of Soviet economic warfare, put it this way: "In dollars and cents, this Russian dumping of aluminum is very costly to American and Canadian aluminum companies and their stockholders. Aluminium Limited's ingot capacity totals 866,000 tons and the United States capacity is about 2 million tons or a total 2.9 million ton capacity. Lowering the price 2 cents a pound reduces possible earnings by $116 million a year — about $55 million after income taxes. Capitalizing this lost earning power at 15 times means a theoretical loss of $825 million in the investment value of aluminum stocks."

In short, a country which only a few years before we had patronized economically as a land of peasants and commissars had acquired in the interval both the means and the knowledge to flex its industrial muscles in a very big way.

However, the real shocker in aluminum was to come not from the U.S.S.R., but from Europe, particularly France.

The French, to be sure, had pioneered in the metal. The ore bauxite was first found in southeast France near the town of Les Baux, from which it was named; and the first ingots were poured in a plant on the outskirts of Paris in 1855. Furthermore, France and the United States had, actually in the same year, 1886, brought into production the reduction process basic to the industry to this day.

But like the automobile, in which the French also pioneered, we had taken over the industry after its initial research and development phase, and at the close of World War II had made of it almost a U. S. and Canadian preserve.

The exclusiveness of the preserve was not to last long. French production began swiftly to mount; so did Norwegian, German, Italian and Swiss. By 1959 French output had surged from 45,000 tons annually to 175,000, with another 125,000 tons scheduled to come in during 1960. Norway had come from almost nothing to 120,000 tons. Even Italy, using the newly discovered natural gas of the Po Valley, was producing 75,000 tons under the skilled hand of Montecatini, one of the chemical giants of Europe and among the best-managed companies on earth.

Furthermore, this European aluminum was competitively — and in the case of France, more than competitively — priced.

Against a United States price in the autumn of 1959 of 24.70 cents a pound, and a Canadian price (for export) of 22.50 cents a pound, French aluminum was being sold at 21.47 cents, German at 23.33 cents and Italian at 27.95 cents. (American and Canadian prices have been marked up even higher since then.)

The European Common Market further aggravated the competitive difficulty posed by European prices.

Early in April of 1959, the magazine *Iron Age,* bible of the metal industries, wrote:

> *The 160 million people now in the six-country Common Market use less than eight pounds of aluminum each annually, as against 21 pounds in the United States. A study of western Europe by one producer for its own use, pegs total consumption at less than one million tons.*
>
> *Most trade observers agree that the per capita consumption*

in the ECM [European Common Market] *is poised to at least double overnight. And on the long term total consumption in western Europe is expected to hit between 1.9 and 2.8 million tons by 1975.*

Today Canadian and United States producers are looking at such a market potential with longing, for obviously the growth in demand is going to increase many times more rapidly in Europe than in the United States. But what the producers see is not encouraging. European prices are competitive, and will become more so. European production might once have faced a bottleneck in electric power, as most of the efficient hydro-power of the Alps has been developed; but the entrance of Norway into the picture and new discoveries of natural gas have changed that.

At Lacq, near the Spanish border, France has brought in a very large gas field which just this year fueled production of 80,000 tons of metal. Other French plants are on drawing boards, and there is at least a chance that the Lacq gas will be piped into Germany in the vicinity of Strasbourg to fuel an increase in German plant.

As for Norway, only 20 per cent of her cheap hydro-power is now developed. Yet even with this amount she had increased aluminum production by 22 per cent in the last year to some 120,000 tons; and this output is almost entirely for export, as only nominal amounts are required for domestic needs.

On top of this, there are new plants coming into production now and planned for the future in the colonial possessions or dominion-associated nations of the European powers — France in the Cameroons, and Belgium in the Congo (although the Congo will soon break its colonial ties). Here in Africa will be made in the future some of the cheapest aluminum on earth. In this production, however, United States and Canadian companies will share.

But it is the tariff situation that really hurts. Import duties on aluminum now vary from none in the Benelux countries to 27 per cent in France, and the common tariff for the whole group under the Treaty of Rome has not yet been set. It is presumed, however, that American and Canadian metal will have to face a barrier on the order of 13 per cent, unless a lower rate can be negotiated through GATT, the General Agreement on Tariffs and Trade. Such a tariff rate will almost seal off the European market to western hemisphere producers, except to the extent that they can share in the African ventures (which, if they are in areas in either colonial or dominion status to the Common Market nations, are within ECM tariff barriers).

Thus, as they look abroad today, what do the big United States and Canadian producers of aluminum see?

They see the great future market for their industry in Europe. But they also see the emergence of an aluminum industry in Europe and European overseas possession which within a decade would have volume sufficient to satisfy this market, and at a price they will be unable to meet. Furthermore, beyond this they see the present 780,000-tons annual output of the Soviet Union mounting, a Russia producing a surplus for export which can be turned loose on the world market at any price that the Kremlin may come to believe will further its economic advantage in a Cold War being fought more and more through the strategy of world trade.

Yet it was only relatively a few years ago that Canada and our Pacific Northwest were in the driver's seat of this fast-growing industry, with the world market apparently at their fingertips. That day passed with the coming into being of the "new" Europe and the winds of new industrial energy blowing over the Russian steppes.

IV

Rebuilt Europe—Competitor and Ally

In the new world scene which emerges today before the eyes of American industry and labor, Europe is at once key and enigma.

We know where we are, as against the Soviet Union, and as against Japan. Japan is a dangerous competitor in our own and many world markets; but there is nothing new in Japanese competition and the problem there is only one of degree. As for the Soviet Union, we know that the new industrial power of that nation will be used against us in the political conflict we call the Cold War. It is power we shall have to counter in our policies on economic aid to the underdeveloped areas, and meet in other ways; but it is an understandable factor. It is a threat — just that — and as such we shall meet and deal with it.

In Europe the situation is more subtle. Huge forces are at work there. In the Common Market, American industry sees both a competitor and an opportunity to gain new markets for itself, as well as an area offering a rich field for investment. But beyond the Common Market — the so-called "Inner Six" — is a larger Europe. There is the Free Trade Area recently organized and signed into a treaty at Stockholm, largely under British leadership — the "Outer Seven," as opposed to the "Inner Six," consisting of Britain, Sweden, Norway, Denmark, Switzerland, Austria and Portugal. And even further beyond are the nations tied economically to Europe, a part of the industrial complex centering today around the heavy industry of the British Midlands, the German Ruhr, France's Lorraine, and Italy's Po Valley: Ireland, Iceland, Greece, Spain, Turkey.

This Europe will play a major, actually a dominant, role in the world economy in the coming decade. It may coalesce into two blocs, tightly knit economically and practicing protectionism against trade with each other, as well as with outside nations. Or it may achieve a larger unity in which the Free Trade Area will slowly merge with the Common Market. It could expand that unity still further, to include the "fringe" nations, eventually even the United States and Canada, thereby becoming an Atlantic Community.

This promises to be the great single story of our times, and the role we choose to play may well tip the balance as between the success or failure of Western civilization.

Yet in this story, it is Europe, not we, which will lay down the line of action, not through a deliberate exercise of economic or political power but simply out of the dynamics of the era brought into being, actually, by our own fear in 1946 of the Soviet Union and its ideological offensive.

Up until World War I, Europe was dominant in industrial society. Its products established the standard for the world. It forged the techniques, did the research, explored the scientific frontiers. With its large accumulation of capital, it exploited the resources of its colonies with low wage rates. This established the basic structure of the nineteenth-century economy, which rested on low-cost labor supplying the industrial nations with raw material.

To this Europe the United States was, prior to 1919, almost an economic colony. Europe furnished in large part the capital to build our railroads and develop our first industrial plant, and at the outbreak of World War I we were still its debtor on balance. To be sure, at that time we were already developing the mass production techniques which have been our particular genius and have built our economic strength, but they were exercised largely in products of European design and invention.

World War I destroyed European supremacy. From that conflict Europe emerged almost as economically prostrate as in 1945. Foreign investments had been liquidated, by confiscation in Germany, and in Britain and France by payments for the large amount of armament, raw materials and foodstuffs imported between 1914 and 1918, much of it from the United States.

Of even greater significance, Europe in 1919 was psychologically exhausted. The blood-letting of the preceding four years, the rapid inflation of currencies and the destruction of industrial plant had had a deadening effect on European economic vitality and imagination.

The old colonial system of the nineteenth century was crumbling. New political ideas were rising, new aspirations flaming in the minds of the underprivileged of the earth. Europe did not comprehend this fully, and tried to rebuild on patterns of the past. In large measure this is why she never recovered the economic strength drained out of her in 1914-18.

The interval between the two world wars saw a measure of European recovery, of course; but it was incomplete and insubstantial. Germany, after going through national bankruptcy by a radical inflation, established a new mark which was strong enough; and for several years Britain clung to a gold standard. But the period between wars saw a steady decline in the value of other currencies of the 1918 combatants, which cut cruelly into living standards — to the benefit only of speculators and American tourists and expatriates who could buy "soft" francs and lire with "hard" dollars.

Furthermore, Germany and England paid tragically in depressed areas and large unemployment for the deflationary policies which maintained the value of the currencies.

All in all, there was a kind of sluttishness about the national economies of Europe from 1918 to 1939 — a softness reflected in fiscal policy, a living from hand to mouth, perhaps a fatigue before the massive energy of the United States, itself as yet but half aware of its new productiveness.

Then the new giant of the West stumbled — badly. The stock market crash of 1929 was followed by a wave of protectionism which took final form in the Hawley-Smoot Tariff Act, vetoed by President Hoover, but passed over his veto into law in 1930. That law with its high tariff walls blocked off the trade by which Europe lived. The Creditanstalt, Vienna's largest bank, failed two years later, and the Great Depression of the 1930's, already holding the United States in its grip, began to spread. Employment declined, factories closed down or operated on short schedules, and the gray half-light of desperation settled on the Continent. This gave the dictators their chance. Mussolini already had capitalized on fears of communism and the deep-seated poverty of Italy. Now Hitler rose to power on the wave of bitterness and political desperation which followed the rise of unemployment in Germany to over 24 per cent of the labor force.

Only in the clash of armaments being rebuilt for the conflict that thoughtful Europeans foresaw as early as 1936 was there any alleviation of industrial stagnation. Then, holocaust again, marking the complete failure, both economic and political, of the old European order.

Thus the fleets of bombers and the battalions of tanks departing the scene in 1945 left a continent in more than physical ruin. They left a whole people bitter, exhausted, disillusioned. And the United States, looking across the North Atlantic, saw the nations from which it had drawn both its racial stocks and its culture poised on the edge of social and economic chaos.

We reacted to this, in a flash of insight and imagination, with the program which General George C. Marshall first outlined on the occasion of his receiving a degree from Harvard in 1946 — the Marshall Plan.

The Marshall Plan was an economic program designed for a political purpose. In 1946 communism enjoyed great prestige in Europe. Stalingrad still stood as the great symbol of the defeat of German arms. The various resistance movements, in which Europe found a much-needed source of pride, had had strong communist affiliations. And communist parties stood ready to make their bid for power, if the economy of the continent could not be rebuilt on capitalist principles. In short, over Europe in 1946 hung a cloud of political uncertainty which raised in this country the specter of communism taking over the whole continent. Suddenly we could see a huge supra-Marxist state spread from the North to the China Seas, to which we would be economically only an appendage.

Nine years later, however, communism in Europe was dead. Even the Marxism of the communist political parties had become in a sense "nationalized," or at least divorced from Kremlin policy. French and Italian communists were first Frenchmen and Italians, and only then Marxists. The political power of the parties had also faded. As a matter of fact, in recent years the political drift of Europe has been more and more to the right.

In large part this was an accomplishment of the Marshall Plan and the aid we furnished under its programs. This American aid did not rebuild Europe — Europeans did that themselves — but it did provide the seed capital without which the rebuilding might have been impossible, or at least dangerously delayed.

All in all, between 1946 and 1955, we furnished the nations of Europe some $26 billion. This was not a great deal, relatively, when spread among eighteen nations over a period of nine years. (It was about what we spent for military aircraft in 1945.) But it was enough. It launched Europe into one of the most remarkable periods of economic growth of all time.

Marshall Plan funds were used in several ways. For instance, they were used to replenish gold stocks and later to stabilize currencies to a degree impossible for any nation except Switzerland between 1918 and 1939. Stabilization did not come all at once. Britain was first, then Germany (which by 1954 had the strongest currency in Europe). The other nations followed, although France not until 1958.

This stability brought about the repatriation of large amounts of liquid capital which had sought refuge abroad during the inflationary cycles of 1918-46, much of it in Switzerland or in other countries through Swiss banks. It was this return of European capital which in large part took European recovery on from where Marshall Plan aid left off, after 1955.

It was Marshall Plan dollars that fed, clothed and heated Europeans for the two years following the German collapse — $4 billion for food and fuel, and another $2.9 billion for needed raw materials to enable factories to get back in production. But from then on, Europe invested ten dollars in production facilities for every dollar from the United States.

In 1955 two giant new rolling mills were turning out 65 per cent of French sheet steel. One third of the financing of these mills came from Marshall Plan aid. Fish products had always been one of Norway's most important industries. It was helped back into production after the war by a United States aircraft carrier anchored in Norwegian waters and converted to a plant to process fish oil. So it went, throughout Europe, the British Midlands, French Lorraine, the German Ruhr, the Italian Po Valley. Between 1946 and 1955: $6.9 billion to Britain . . . $5.1 billion to France . . . $3.8 billion to West Germany . . . $2.6 billion to Italy . . . eighteen nations in all received seed capital.

American aid has at times been criticized, on the grounds that it went for the most part to large firms, and because its administrators attached too many strings, demanding that it be spent on certain items of U. S. export. But the proof of the dish was in the eating, and today no one in Europe except the most stubborn critic of the United States has in retrospect anything but gratitude and admiration for our aid.

Furthermore, the rapidity of European recovery was remarkable. Even though Germany was still economically supine in 1949, the total production of the continent had already climbed back to equal prewar levels. Between 1948 and 1957, when the European Common Market was put into treaty form, the gross output of product on a per capita basis rose by 40 per cent, as against a rise in this country and Canada of 25 per cent. More recently, 1950-59, gross national product in Europe has risen a total of 75 per cent, roughly three times the rise in the United States.

In the four years following 1953, the ownership of passenger cars in Europe increased by 50 per cent, and of household appliances by 72 per cent. The over-all total personal spending on goods and services rose by 5 per cent a year, and by 1957 the average European was enjoying a standard of living about equal to that of the United States in the mid-1920's.

This "new" Europe, immeasurably stronger in relation to the rest of the world than it had been in thirty years, had by now aligned itself squarely with the United States. It stood with us as an ally against the Soviet Union in the Cold War, which was more and more becoming an economic conflict. The success of the Marshall Plan was complete.

In that very success, however, we were soon to find that we had aided in building up more than an economic and political ally against the Soviet Union. We had also helped bring into being a competitor in the world markets — markets which during World War II had come to us almost by default as Europe had found herself shut off from her traditional overseas outlets or unable to serve them from her war-strained industrial base.

Within a few short years German and British salesmen in Latin America, Africa, Asia were busy recapturing what they had lost. In this they were aided by the fact that the cost of goods made in relatively low-wage Europe was in many lines far lower than ours. In the world market we were being underpriced. And not only in the world markets; the bite of European competition was beginning to hurt here at home.

The trade patterns of the world were changing swiftly, dramatically. Nor was this only because of Europe. Across the Pacific a long-time competitor of American industry had made as spectacular a recovery as Europe. Japan too was reaching out to regain lost markets, threatening the postwar trade supremacy of the United States.

The economic realities of the 1950's were beginning to hit American industry and labor.

V

The Rebuilding of Japan

WORLD WAR II crumbled the economic strength of Japan even more than that of Europe. In addition to the physical destruction of plant and the surrender of foreign markets, Japan lost an empire from which she had been drawing the raw materials to support her industrial life. At the close of the war, territory under Japanese control had shrunk by 52 per cent; and a nation that lived by manufacturing and export was without the wherewithal to feed its factories and support its trade.

At the same time, Japan experienced a population increase from 71 million in 1938 to 80 million in 1948 as colonists were repatriated from her former colonial possessions. These people were crowded into the home islands on a land area equal roughly to that of California, only 17 per cent of which was arable. Add to this a birth rate among the world's highest and it becomes evident that no nation of modern times, not even defeated Germany in 1945, ever faced a more serious economic problem than did postwar Japan.

In the first three years following the close of hostilities little was done except to keep Japan breathing industrially. This was the period of Allied control and American direct aid, when occupation forces supervised the economy

and instituted many reforms — among them the breaking
up of the big trading corporations which in the prewar years
had given Europe and the United States such stiff competition in markets over much of the earth.

A country which lives by export, Japan in those three years
could export only a trickle of goods, these largely from ac-
cumulated stocks; and the result was that spending for
rehabilitation triggered a violent inflation of the yen.

In 1948, the United States saw in Japan a danger twin to
that seen two years earlier in Europe: the chance of communism moving in and taking over in an economy almost
prostrate in a political void. But again we reacted with imagination, this time with the mission headed by Joseph M.
Dodge, a Detroit banker, former financial adviser to General
MacArthur and subsequently Director of the Budget in the
United States.

The Dodge commission stabilized the yen, eliminated
many government controls which were choking back economic growth, and halted deficit financing. With the basis
laid for sound currency, Japan began again to move into
world trade, with startling success. In one year, 1948-49, production jumped by 25 per cent, a rise kept rolling by some
$2 billion in aid furnished in the next two years by the
United States.

However, it was the Korean War which really cemented
Japanese recovery. During that war Japan earned large
amounts of foreign exchange through the sales of $3 billion
in goods and services to the Allied forces in the Far East and
to the American forces in her home islands. A great out-
burst in industrial activity followed, which in turn resulted
in rising prices. This for a time threatened to price Japan
out of those markets she was just in process of rewinning.
Furthermore, the economy was in a precarious position due
to its reliance upon U. S. military spending, soon to be de-
creased. But in this secondary, minor inflationary crisis

which came to a head in 1953, Japan herself acted swiftly with deflationary countermeasures. Credit was tightened, particularly for export transactions, and after a short period of not unpainful deflation, Japan moved into the extraordinary boom that has marked her economy in recent years.

The first phase of this boom came between the beginning of 1954 and the end of 1955, a period marked by heavy domestic investment in modernizing plant, the elimination of weaker enterprises and a major effort to diversify existing export markets and to develop new ones. Progress was also made in improving Japan's international payments position, and the rise in foreign trade allowed a build-up in foreign exchange reserves.

In 1956 Japan entered the final phase of economic recovery. Trade continued to increase and broaden, living standards rose at home, production rose sharply and capital began to flow overseas. There was a slight downturn in 1957 and 1958, but the setback was temporary. Today Japan, her industrial plant rebuilt, has taken again her place among the important industrial powers, with a record of an 8 per cent average annual growth since the war in gross national product, the highest in the world. In 1958 Japan's total output was 50 per cent above 1940, which gave her people a living standard about 25 per cent higher than in 1938.

Such economic growth has stabilized the political scene in Japan. Since World War II the communists have talked much, and even to some extent infiltrated SOHOYO, the nation's most important labor federation. But they are now plowing unproductive ground, and the country seems firmly committed to the political West.

On the other hand, Japan's economy lacks the rich diversification of Europe or the United States, and a strong group which thinks in terms of traditional trade ties with the Orient, which means Red China, is inclined to present the communist states in the best possible light.

The future of Japan, much more than that of Europe, rests with outside nations, particularly the United States. This is because of her economic dependence on foreign trade. For instance, Japan's exports to the rest of the world dropped from $1.3 billion in 1951 to $1.2 billion in 1952 and in 1953. The drop was only $100 million. Yet even this shading of export volume drove Japan's deficit on foreign account up from $641 million to $1.1 billion in two years.

The largest companies in the United States and Europe are either financial, such as insurance companies, or manufacturers. In Japan they are the big trading corporations. Yawata Iron & Steel, for instance, with an annual volume of $340 million, is the largest manufacturer in Japan. But two trading companies, Mitsui Bussan and Mitsubishi Shoji, each do over a billion; and there are five others whose annual volume exceeds that of the iron and steel products firm.

This heavy reliance on foreign trade leaves the economy of Japan extremely susceptible to moves which tend either to expand or to decrease her trade with Europe and the United States.

The European Common Market, for instance, will have a profound influence on Japanese industry. So will the Free Trade Area signed into treaty in Stockholm in the autumn of 1959. In a manner as yet undetermined, these blocs will reach deep into Japanese economic life. So with the often arbitrary actions on tariffs and quotas of the United States.

We have won Japan to the West by a program of economic assistance not very dissimilar from that used to prevent the spread of communism in Europe. But whereas in Europe the cause has been won, barring some unforeseeable economic tragedy, in Japan we must still work at it. This does not mean more aid: Japan today is capable of carrying her own economic weight. She is even exporting capital to such an extent that in 1959 she became for the first time in her history a creditor nation. What Japan must have is the freedom and opportunity to trade. Her goods are low-cost, for her wages are the lowest of any modern industrial nation, and those goods in the market places of the world represent competition hard for the United States and Europe to meet. But those same goods must be allowed a market. They must not be shut out by discriminatory quotas and tariffs. If they are, all that has been accomplished in Japan — and with that, our foothold in Asia — will be swept away through our own shortsightedness.

The consequence of this could be catastrophic.

In Europe today there is less fear of the Soviet Union, either militarily or economically, than in the United States. There are perhaps several reasons for this. For one thing, Europe lives so close to Soviet military power that it must assume that that power will not be employed against it, as an individual must assume that on stepping from his house he will not be killed by an automobile. Except in a philosophic sense, nations as well as people must assume that life will not be terminated overnight.

But Europe's lack of alarm at Soviet power has one very realistic base. This is the belief that it is Red China and the Soviet Union who are the "natural" antagonists, that as the fire of revolutionary fervor diminishes in Russia, and perhaps increases in China, geophysical-economic factors will cause those nations to clash. In the chancelleries of Europe, men looking ahead see the enormous population pressure of China, and the need for raw materials that the growing industry of that nation will need. They see also, just to the north, the huge, unsettled land mass of Siberia, an area rich in natural resources. European newspapermen returning from behind the Bamboo Curtain report that the frontier of outer Mongolia is the tightest on earth.

In short, the "Yellow Peril," so beloved of sensational journalism fifty years ago and a favorite specter of Wilhelm II in pre-World War I Germany, may in the next thirty years become very much a reality. Some European observers can even see the day when a Europeanized Russia will be allied with the rest of Europe to resist the rise of a new threat in Asia — a bid for world power by the Red Chinese.

The role of Japan in such an eventuality is, obviously, of the greatest importance. Japan alone is a modern economic power in Asia. Skilled now in techniques, and possessed of great industrial vitality, Japan is currently attempting to carve out for herself a position in the community of free nations. If this opportunity is denied her by arbitrary restrictions imposed upon the exports by which she lives, she may well turn back to the concept of herself as leader in a co-prosperity sphere in Asia. Indeed, if the markets of the world are closed off to Japanese goods she might have no choice.

Political ideologies in the modern world are becoming more and more flexible to economics, to the need of nations and people to eat and live. And the prospect of a Red China rising to power with its half-billion population under Japanese industrial development and Japanese economic direction is not remote. It is a possibility the West must guard against, and work to avoid.

This is but one of the new economic currents that underlie the world today; but it is one fraught with explosive potential, and the problems it creates will in the next decade come home to roost on the doorstep of American workers and industry alike. In fact, in many industries it is already with us, in the rising volume of imports to this country that bear the label: *Made in Japan.*

VI

Competition Begins to Hurt

For the American people 1957 was a historic year. During the previous decade the underlying sweep of economic events had held two main stories: the industrial rebuilding of Europe and Japan to a point where production and income exceeded even the prewar years, and the amazing resiliency and strength shown by the American economy, which passed through two minor recessions without the deflationary spiraling that had turned recession into deep depression so often in the past. These were the brilliant achievements of the postwar years.

To be sure, one great problem remained on which no progress had been made, that of the underdeveloped areas. But so far this was a story with only a beginning. Like the poor who are traditionally always with us, the problems of the poorer nations of the world will have to be lived with by the industrial areas of Europe and the United States for decades to come. For years the ingenuity and political skill of the best minds of the West will be taxed to cope with the massive poverty of Asia, Africa and parts of Latin America.

But the over-all look of the economic situation in 1957 was good. We could now almost certainly count on never again having to go through a depression like that of the 1930's.

Moreover, both our flanks had been strengthened economically to the point that communism was a threat now only in the underdeveloped areas — and therefore remote at the moment. A prosperous Europe and a thriving Japan seemed to hem in the Soviet Union economically as effectively as our Strategic Air Command had contained that nation militarily before the bomber surrendered precedence to the missile and the preponderance of air power passed from the West.

This was a year in which we could look back with pride on a period of great accomplishment, a time for the prideful flexing of industrial muscles, for saying to ourselves and our allies, "Well done," and then sitting back to relax. We were shortly to be disillusioned and to learn that the swift-paced movement of economics today allows no weariness and permits no rest; for in the very successes of 1946-57 we had in fact already opened a Pandora's box from which were emerging new problems destined to test our resourcefulness in the future even more, perhaps, than had the difficulties of the past.

Since the invention of the sewing machine, the Singer Manufacturing Company had dominated its field. For 108 years it sold its machines throughout the world. Singer salesmen traveled by donkey, camel, horseback throughout Africa, the Australian bush, the interior of China. Singer had sold over 1.5 million machines to the Japanese by 1930. It had pioneered in bringing to many people their first experience with American merchandising methods: a mass-produced product sold with trade-in allowance, and on terms. In its industry, Singer was top company, so much so that, as the magazine *Business Week* put it in an article on Singer in 1957: "Singer Mfg. Co. never quite believed competition could hurt."

But in the years following World War II, Singer found that competition could hurt, and badly.

Its first warning of trouble came after the war when the Italians and Germans began selling the new zigzag machines, Necchi and Pfaff. Yet Singer simply raised its eyebrows at the new European machines, even though their design made black-model Singers look like something out of an 1890 mail order catalogue. Then the Japanese moved in and soon were all over the world with a low-priced model underselling Singer.

This caused White, the second largest manufacture in the United States, to throw in the sponge on domestic manufacture and turn to selling a machine here made entirely in Japan. But by then Singer was on its postwar feet and moving fast to firm its position in the world markets.

Its first move was to start importing here zigzag machines from its European plants. But despite this move, Singer had by mid-1958 seen its share of the domestic market for home machines drop from 66 per cent (prewar) to around 33 per cent. Furthermore, Singer executives were also aware that their great future markets lay abroad. Most Americans already had a sewing machine. But in other areas of the world, rising living standards were building a market so far only scratched. Actually, by 1958 foreign sales were already providing 60 per cent of total income, and the company set about to reorganize its production setup with this in mind.

Singer put a plant in Australia. In Japan it bought a half interest in the Pine Sewing Machine Manufacturing Company, Ltd., which sells both to the local Japanese and to the Southeast Asian markets. The company's existing plants in France, Italy and Germany were assigned to produce special models for the European Common Market. In Germany, Singer began to acquire shares of its licensee, Naehmaschinenfabrik, Karlsruhe.

Many problems proved stubborn, however. In Canada, Singer had had almost a monopoly before World War II, but by 1958 it held only half the market, a third having been

lost to the Japanese. In Mexico, it was touch and go, with
new competition coming from the Japanese Toyoda, actually
an imitation of the Singer. In Brazil, Singer was also losing
ground, again to the Japanese, trying to sell a model priced
some 20 per cent above its competitors.

India too presented a problem with local companies reported to be planning to ship 50,000 machines a year to the
United States, while Red China was making and marketing a machine to sell at cut-rate prices throughout Southeast Asia. Only in France was Singer really secure, where
behind high tariff barriers it still held 85 per cent of the market through its facilities at Bonnières-sur-Seine.

Then, in November of 1959, Singer announced a broad
reshuffling of its entire production facilities. All industrial
manufacture was moved out of its Bridgeport, Conn., plant
and distributed among plants at Clydebank in Scotland
(long the producer for the British Isles), Karlsruhe in Germany and Elizabethport, N. J. The shift was to be carried
out in stages, scheduled to be completed by 1964. By that
year, Singer will be producing 45 per cent of its industrial
machines at Clydebank, 20 per cent at Karlsruhe and 35
per cent in New Jersey.

All needles will be made abroad. As for home sewing
machines, only the more expensive models will be made in
the United States. Cheaper models will be brought in from
foreign factories.

Thus the Singer Manufacturing Company, cash-rich, experienced in foreign operations and managerially skilled,
moved to adapt itself to the new economic tides which today flow back and forth across the world as the result of the
emergence of an industrially reinvigorated Europe and
Japan. Singer was one of the first to find itself face to face
with realities bred in the postwar years.

But it was by no means alone. The same facts of life were
becoming apparent in many industries.

In 1954 one out of seven portable typewriters sold in the United States was of foreign manufacture; today imports account for nearly half.

American manufacturers of bicycles, driven hard by the European competition, are holding some 70 per cent of the American market only by importing chains, brakes, spokes, tires and saddles, and combining these with frames made here on assembly line runs. European cameras are coming into the American market, and many of American manufacture now are assembled from parts made abroad.

When we have thought in the past of foreign competition, it has been in terms of price and of lower-cost labor in Europe and Japan. But in many lines today the competitive factor is not only price. Price hurt Singer's position in the domestic and world markets, but so did the superior design and equally fine workmanship of the Italian and West German products.

The inroads of the European automobile into the American market are only partly due to price; the functional approach of European designers and in many instances a better product were equally strong factors in the rise of auto imports to some 10 per cent of the American market in 1959. So was it in the case of typewriters and bicycles. Even in the area of distribution, where it was long our vanity that American techniques stood alone, we are today beginning to be challenged. American electronics manufacturers looking abroad for new plant keep comfortably in the south of Europe, for in the north lies Philips of Eindhoven in the Netherlands, which is believed to have the world's most efficient marketing and distribution organization.

Japan too is coming up fast and hard, and again not solely on the basis of price or in the traditional items of Japanese exports — cotton cloth, gloves and the wide variety of low-priced goods found on the counters of chain stores.

Japan is selling 38 per cent of the stainless steel tableware sold in this country, which, it is estimated, has cost the industry about 3000 jobs in the five-year period ending with 1959. In the past six years, Japan has increased her share of our domestic plywood market, at a cost here of 11,000 jobs.

Roughly half the small transistor radios sold in the United States today are of Japanese manufacture; and one firm, Motorola, last year announced for the West Coast of the United States a new factory which would assemble small radios entirely of Japanese parts.

The United States' volume of exports of manufactured goods was still rising — up to 1958, that is. But this was a result of the rising tide of world trade. The significant thing was that our imports were increasing much faster than our exports. Imports of goods from abroad rose by 77 per cent between 1953 and 1958, while our exports rose by only 27 per cent. It was the trend that mattered, and the trend as early as 1953-54 was turning against us.

We had cooperated with money and support in the rebuilding of the economies of Japan and Europe in order to secure those areas against a drift to communism. But in so doing, we had brought a new balance of economic power of the West into being. No longer did the United States dollar rule alone in the financial centers of the world, and in many markets American goods were losing their competitive edge.

VII

Typewriters, Tape, and the Treaty of Rome

THE POSTWAR WAVE of investment in foreign plant by American firms predates 1957, the year that the European Common Market became a reality in the Treaty of Rome. Today, due to the ECM, that wave promises to reach tidal proportions. A survey made by the Department of Commerce in early 1959 found that out of 1000 top executives of American corporations, over 88 per cent were either considering or had under way plans for the expansion of plant overseas.

The earlier investment, however, sprang from quite different motives from those which are sending American firms abroad today. Royal McBee, for instance, manufacturers of typewriters and other office machinery, first went to Holland in 1953. The Common Market was at that time only a dream in the minds of a few European economists. Royal's reason for going to Holland was that Europe was then short of hard currency, and the company thought it could assemble a few typewriters from American parts and sell them on the spot. Assembly requires a good deal of labor, and labor in Europe was cheap.

The company rented a plant in Leiden formerly used in cotton manufacture, went to work and by early 1954 had approximately 160 Dutch employees. The operation was successful and was expanded — first, to the simpler phases of manufacture; then as volume built up, to complete production, both assembly and the manufacture of parts. Employment at Leiden increased tenfold, and a second and then a third building were added. The company is now building an entirely new factory on a ten-acre site outside the city and another plant is under construction at Cuyk.

Production figures on Royal's foreign operation are not revealed, but the company is believed to have already produced over 500,000 machines in Holland. From plant there it is selling both in the European and world market. What is even more significant, Royal will import into the United States from Holland a new Royalite portable. With this machine it hopes to hold its position in the portable market in the United States, which has been so aggressively invaded by the European makers in the past few years.

Minnesota Mining and Manufacturing Company had somewhat different motives in opening abroad. The famed "3M" is a company of spectacular growth — its stock has increased in value over the last ten years by better than twenty times. Its best-known product is "Scotch" tape. But, research-minded and always searching aggressively for new products, the company has branched out into coated abrasives, roofing granules, fluorocarbons, electrical products and chemicals. Its Graphic Products Division (Thermo-Fax duplicating machines) is currently its fastest-growing line. A measure of its success can be had from the fact that since the period 1947-49 the total output of goods and services of this country has increased by 75 per cent, whereas 3M sales have risen by 257 per cent.

The company moved into foreign markets in 1951, and 1952 was its first full year of foreign operations. In that year 3M's foreign sales amounted to $20 million. They reached roughly $90 million in 1959.

The firm now has fourteen manufacturing plants in ten

foreign countries, eight in Europe, three in Latin America, and one each in Canada, Australia and the Union of South Africa. It has recently signed an agreement with a Japanese firm for the establishment of a subsidiary. Foreign sales today are roughly 20 per cent of gross.

While the company exports from the United States, it regards its foreign plants as the basic strength of its foreign operations.

Lower costs abroad do not seem to be a significant factor in 3M's foreign plant expansion, or at least not to the degree motivating other firms. Currency exchange difficulties, the existence or threat of tariff barriers and the maintaining of its patent position (an important factor in a firm expanding through new products) are given by the company as the principal reasons for its present large investment in foreign plant. Nor has foreign competition been a deciding factor in 3M's decisions, as was the case with Singer; 3M was simply an aggressive company which, as it developed new products, and as its older products came to saturate more and more the domestic market, began to look for new markets. It found these, in greatest potential, overseas.

Royal and 3M thus branched into foreign manufacture more or less for a historical reason: the search for new markets, which in their case could be served most effectively from foreign plant. To be sure, in the case of Royal, there were the exchange difficulties more or less peculiar to the post-World War II years. But by and large these companies expanded overseas for the same reason that so many other American corporations had done so in the past: United Shoe Machinery, Norton of Worcester (abrasives), American Optical, International Business Machines, Gillette and the dozens of other manufacturing companies whose foreign investment had supplemented that of such producers of raw materials as the oil and mining companies in the large stake abroad which American industry had in 1955.

Such firms stand to benefit greatly from the fact that they were entrenched in Europe before the Common Market came into being. But this is due either to luck or to extraordinary foresight. For it was not until the Treaty of Rome that the message was written clearly for everyone to see. It was then that the wave of interest in foreign plant really began to build up, as many corporate executives, who until then had devoted their entire energy to building up domestic plant and sales, saw that it was now Europe if they wanted to expand, even to maintain present position, or in some cases even to stay alive.

Actually, however, the shadow of the ECM began to loom over Europe as early as 1946. Even then the best minds on the Continent began to see that some kind of European unity was a necessity if the continent was to avoid those internecine wars which had written the most tragic chapters of Europe's past.

Furthermore, the belief was growing that such unity could be achieved only through economic means. The lessons of the 1920's and 1930's were there for everyone to see — the failures of the old League of Nations, of Locarno, the burying of Aristide Briand's dreams of United Europe. The animosities of centuries could not be buried through political approach, not even through common defense measures in the face of the Soviet threat. It is significant that the only effort toward unity since World War II that failed completely was the European Defense Community, which went on the rocks when it failed of ratification by the French parliament because it carried with it a surrender of political independence and control of individual national security to which France would not agree.

On the other hand, as Europe moved in stages toward unity through economic measures, each step met with success.

In 1948, Belgium, Holland and Luxembourg founded

the customs union called Benelux. There followed, under United States sponsorship, the Organization for European Economic Cooperation (OEEC), a seventeen-nation plan to organize Marshall Plan aid. Then came the European Payments Union (EPA), a clearinghouse for European foreign payments and financial account. In 1952 came the European Coal and Steel Community. And finally Euratom — the treaty which, signed concurrently with the Rome Treaty, pooled resources to develop the commercial use of atomic energy. The only successful noneconomic step toward unity in the whole postwar period, it should be noted, was the North Atlantic Treaty Organization, which committed the United States to cementing the military power of the West against the massed divisions of Soviet power in the East.

During these years the United States, speaking at first with all the authority that our Marshall Plan lent us, was continually urging economic unity in Europe. We pointed at ourselves as the splendid example. What, we asked in effect, was the secret of our extraordinary growth, our present riches? To be sure, to some extent our good fortune rested on the huge storehouse of raw materials that we had inherited on the North American continent. But our real secret was that in the United States lay the greatest single free market on earth.

Here on half a continent were 179 million people whose industrial activity was hampered by no trade barriers. Here was an area producing an infinite variety of goods free to flow to their natural markets, an area where labor enjoyed complete mobility and where capital could find that region in which it could be most profitably employed. This was the prime reason for our high living standards in an age when mass markets must exist to justify that mass production which alone could bring consumers' goods down to a mass price. Here was the real key to our industrial genius, the secret of the "American way."

To all of this, Europe listened and, in the Treaty of Rome, signified its agreement. We had made our point.

The European Common Market, which the Treaty brought into being, set up the following objectives:

To expand the size of the European market so that companies could attain the size necessary for maximum efficiency in mass production.

To expand the labor market, and to give it flexibility and mobility.

To promote the flow of capital in order to stimulate growth in the less advanced areas of Europe and also associated territories overseas.

To attract more foreign capital, especially from the United States, this because of the wider protected market that would be open to a plant set up within the European community.

To widen the area of competition in Europe, which would force the production of goods in the most suitable areas by the most efficient firms.

The treaty which addressed the six countries of Europe's industrial core to these broad ends is a complicated one, but its main provisions are as follows:

(1) Tariffs and quotas and other barriers to trade as between the six signatory nations would be eliminated over a period of twelve to fifteen years (a period subsequently shortened).

(2) Concurrently and in conformity with the General Agreement on Tariffs and Trade, a single tariff schedule would be set up between the six nations and the rest of the world. Also the six would operate as a unit in negotiating commercial policies with other nations.

(3) All restrictions on the movement of services, labor, capital and business enterprises between the six nations would be abolished and payments would be free to the extent required to make this effective.

(4) Cartels and private trade restraining devices would be prohibited unless they contributed to improvements in production and distribution, or to technical or economic progress.

(5) The members would agree to coordinate monetary and fiscal policy with the purpose of achieving in each country balance in the over-all international payments, high employment and general price stability.

(6) A common agricultural policy would be established within the community.

(7) Investment funds were to be established, one to operate in Europe, and one to operate in the overseas territories of the six nations.

There were many other provisions in the treaty. One provided for temporary postponement of tariff reductions where the adjustment forced by the reduction would be too severe. A social fund was to be established to help relieve the possible economic hardship to workers in industry hurt by the liberalizing of trade. The overseas colonies and associated territories of the six signing nations were included within the structure of the Common Market, unless any of them themselves decided otherwise. And there were provisions for establishing the principle of equal pay for equal work for women and men throughout the community and the harmonizing of overtime pay on the French standard.

Beyond these specific stipulations, the members formulated the high purpose of improving working conditions for labor, and improving living standards.

These are the main economic provisions of the European Common Market, and as such they are the factors of the most immediate concern to businessmen and workers in the United States.

It would be a mistake, however, to regard the market as being only this, a treaty of economic impact, a commercial or economic coalescing of nations which intend to remain essentially independent. The research and policy committee of the Committee for Economic Development pointed out in 1958 that the economic provisions of the Treaty of Rome go far beyond trade liberalization and "have profound political implications. A real surrender of sovereignty is required. Common Market institutions, legislative, executive, and judicial, will be established with authority to make and carry out policy in certain matters. They will operate, in part, by majority vote, not by unanimity. It is possible that they may in the future be partly directly elected by the people, not chosen by the governments of the member states.

"More important than any specific provisions, the Treaty . . . reflects a new nationalism of Western Europe — or of Little Europe — as distinct from the nationalism of France or Germany or Italy. This new nationalism has not displaced the old nationalisms but rather has been superimposed upon them."

VIII
Investment in Europe Becomes a Trek

EARLY IN SEPTEMBER of 1959, the Reece Corporation of Waltham, Mass., sent to its stockholders a letter announcing the firm's intention to manufacture its product abroad. Reece is the oldest name in the manufacture of certain special machines for the garment industry. The company was founded in 1881, and over the years has built a world-wide market for its buttonhole- and pocket-making machinery. Its sales and service facilities reach throughout Africa, Latin America, Europe, the Far East. This foreign volume had become so important a part of gross that Reece had been considering the building of a plant abroad for some time.

In the ECM, however, Reece management saw a threat that had to be met quickly. The firm's competition was coming for the most part from plants in West Germany which paid wage rates roughly one-third of those at Reece's United States plant. Furthermore, the company saw that, with the ECM, the time was almost at hand when its German competitors would be within ECM tariff walls, when German machines could be sold duty-free throughout the six nations, whereas Reece would face a tariff barrier common to all the six. Such a tariff hurdle, on top of current wage differentials, meant for Reece one thing: a factory in Europe, or the surrendering of its continental market.

In addition, licenses to import would not be a problem for machinery made within the ECM, and exports to South America and other dollar-tight areas would be much facilitated by European plant.

In the winter of 1958, Reece made a careful survey of all countries within the ECM, and chose Holland — specifically, after visiting many communities, the old Dutch city of Leiden. Dutch engineers were employed, a plant site acquired, and by the fall of 1959 construction was well under way toward an opening planned for 1960. Reece chose Holland because its management liked the Dutch people and the attitude of both government and labor toward industry.

It found that in Holland maximum as well as minimum wages are established, and that all rates are set by mutual agreement among labor, industry and government under the economic reality that Dutch industry must stay competitive. Some 40 per cent of Holland's total output goes into export each year.

At first Reece will only serve the ECM market from its Dutch plant. Later it may widen the area to include Britain, perhaps, and the rest of Europe, possibly eventually much of its world market outside the United States.

Thus was the company forced to abandon its seventy-five-year policy of manufacturing only at home plant in this country. It had to have plant abroad, and so built plant abroad; and the jobs created by this new investment were in Holland, not in the United States.

Meanwhile, not far from Leiden, in the Dutch town of Amersfoort, a neighboring firm of Reece in Waltham was building its first European factory. High Voltage Engineering, however, had been led to European plant for somewhat different reasons. This was a new industry, manufacturing large particle accelerators used to produce radiation synthetically. High Voltage equipment sells for between

$20,000 and $1,000,000 a machine, and it is used by university and government laboratories in basic research — its supervoltage X-rays, for instance, in cancer therapy and industrial radiography.

High Voltage had been in business only eleven years when, in 1958, it found that it was already doing roughly half its business abroad. It went to Europe for this reason, and because the technology of Europe is skilled and the interest in research wide. Labor cost was a factor here too, but perhaps a lesser one. To be able to sell in European currencies and to service European installations from plant in Europe were other advantages.

These are but random examples of the trek that by this time was on. The chemical companies who murmur about protection in this country are as a rule none too communicative about their operations overseas, but Monsanto was hiding none of its foreign plans under a bushel basket.

The International Division of this company was formed only in 1953, but in the five-year interval up to 1958 its combined exports and production abroad had risen from $64 million to $140 million. With total investment in foreign plant at $500 million in 1959, Monsanto was in that year selling 20 per cent of its output overseas.

Du Pont, whose foreign production had been confined to Canada and Latin America, was thrusting across the Atlantic with three plants, in Northern Ireland, the Netherlands and Belgium. Union Carbide early in 1959 announced its third plant in Europe in Belgium. Olin Mathieson had a foothold in West Germany. Allied Chemical was planning production in Europe. American Cyanamid and Dow were also pushing aggressively into foreign operations.

As between companies, the reasons for such expansion varied. Monsanto, for instance, believed that with the development in Europe of an American-type mass market, demand for chemicals there would rise sharply. Another company believed that to compete in Europe with European chemical firms was hopeless, but that Europe represented an economically sound base from which to manufacture for the Latin American market. A third company was building plants across the Atlantic simply to hang on to its present $15 million in foreign sales.

Wages in the chemical industry are not as big a factor of cost as in most other industries. Yet the differential as between Europe and the United States — roughly 1 to 4 — certainly weighed in the decisions of such companies to increase investment in foreign plant. Then too, the necessary outlay in Europe was lower: factories there cost 10 to 20 per cent less to build and equip than in the United States.

It is, as a matter of fact, easy to overemphasize the importance of the present wage differential. It exists today and is important today; but American executives realize that over a period of time wages will rise in Europe, not only absolutely but in relation to the level in the United States. Dr. Carlo Calosi, vice-president for Europe of the Raytheon Company, whose business is electronics, missiles and radar, warned in the fall of 1959, for instance, that corporations would be making a mistake if they based their decisions to build plant abroad on a differential existing today.

Yet Raytheon itself by 1959 had moved importantly into Europe. With a subsidiary of the giant Italian Edison, it had developed and engineered in Rome its new large ship radar, brought out in competition with the British firm of Decca. It had licensing arrangements in Naples with other Italian interests. And at Palermo in Sicily it held an interest with still another Italian firm in a plant manufacturing microwave tubes which, interestingly enough, it could land in the United States, duty and freight paid, for some 20 per cent less than it could manufacture the same tube in its domestic plants.

But Raytheon with its highly skilled management was

looking beyond the immediate cost differential as between Italy (where its foreign operations are centered) and the United States. The company had had a spectacular record of growth — its sales rose from $111 million in 1952 to over $480 million in 1959 — but the rise had been in large part attributable to defense orders. With 85 per cent of its gross dependent on the weapon use of its product, Raytheon was thinking in terms of developing its nondefense business. And that meant, to the big electronics firm, an expansion of European plant. Like other American firms it saw Europe beginning to build the kind of mass production-mass consumption market that spelled opportunity — the kind of opportunity that American business could understand.

At the core of this was the European Common Market, the Inner Six of France, Germany, Italy and the Benelux nations, the heart of industrial Europe. In 1957 this core, representing the formerly fragmented national economies of the six, was just beginning to coalesce. Here was a population of 161 million of the most culturally advanced and technically skilled people on earth. Circumstances had delayed the development of their industrial and economic potential. But now the handcuffs of economic nationalism had been broken, and their present combined $125 billion of gross national product was headed for a steep increase. Furthermore, outside this core of the Inner Six, Britain was already moving toward a second bloc, the so-called Free Trade Area consisting of Britain, Norway, Sweden, Denmark, Switzerland and Austria (later Portugal was to be included). And beyond this was still another potential free trade area or bloc: Iceland, Ireland, Greece, Turkey, Finland and Spain.

There were many hurdles — even within the original Inner Six — to be overcome, and there still are. But industrialists looking far ahead could see the possibility of the emergence, over the next fifteen to twenty years, of a huge

Free Europe, a single economy of continental nations and those outlying nations tied to the Continent by tradition and trade, which would have a population of 360 million by 1970 — twice that of the Soviet Union in 1958 — and a gross national product which by the same year would roughly equal that of the United States today.

There were in 1957, and there still are, many divisions of opinion on this longer-range projection of European unity, and we may never see it quite realized. But the fact remains that in 1957 when the Treaty of Rome was signed, enormous possibilities were opened to American business. And American firms began to move fast — so fast that by December of 1959 the *Wall Street Journal* in a lead article could write:

> *The drift of American corporations into Europe's nascent Common Market is turning into a stampede.*
>
> *Yanks already on the scene are waving newcomers on, asserting profits are more prodigious and marketing prospects more pregnant than back home . . .*
>
> *The transatlantic sprint is occurring in a spirit often approaching gaiety.*

The story of TV in Italy is an illustration of the why and wherefore of the "stampede."

Italian manufacturers were in 1958 turning out some 400,000 sets a year for a market with a projected growth potential of some 20 per cent annually. The Italians, however, were for the most part assemblers, using largely imported components — roughly 50 per cent from northern Europe, and 50 per cent from United States firms like RCA, General Electric and Westinghouse.

Such parts, from both Europe and the United States, had to come into Italy over a wall of tariff and other duties of approximately 30 per cent. But under the provisions of the ECM that wall would be dropped over a period of years until, eventually, tubes from northern Europe would enter duty-free, while those from the United States would still face whatever common tariff the six nations agreed among themselves to maintain. And in January of 1959 the first reduction was in fact made, and Italian duties went down by 3 per cent.

But Philips of Holland, the toughest kind of competitor, had decided not to wait for the advantage it would enjoy with the ECM in final form — entry to Italy duty-free. In September of 1959 the Dutch company opened plant in Italy, and at once dropped its tube price from $29 to $22.50.

The results were dramatic, said a *Wall Street Journal* report which went on to quote an American competitor as saying, "In this situation it's almost impossible for us to sell." The forecast at that time was that the sale of tubes in Italy from the United States would drop in the following year by 80 per cent.

The only answer possible for American firms was foreign plant — Sylvania was already in Milan with a 50 per cent interest in an Italian firm. At least one other large tube manufacturer had by late 1959 completed a survey of Common Market nations and the final decision as to investment in European plant was in the hands of top management in the United States. Admiral, already assembling in Milan, was looking for additional plant.

Philco was also moving in fast. In late 1958 the company was only making preliminary studies, but the following July it announced the formation of Philco Italiana. By the close of 1959 it had two factories in operation, one manufacturing radios and TV sets, another refrigerators, and both factories were being expanded to include washing machines.

But the most significant development in 1957-58 was that the purpose of much European plant was changing. Originally American firms built abroad largely to manufacture for the market in the country where they put their factories.

Later the purpose became broader, to serve not only a local market but that of all Common Market Europe. But now corporations were seeing even wider horizons for their foreign operations. Europe had been found a cheap base on which to manufacture, in certain (although by no means all) lines cheaper than the United States; and firms with plant there realized that it was with this production they could best serve the world market.

Philco, for instance, will produce at its new Italian plant for its customers throughout the Middle East. Thus more than production for Italy and other Common Market countries was lost to the company's plants back in the United States.

Even beyond this, more and more firms were looking still further ahead to the time when European plant would be used to import back into the United States. Edwin Hartrich, an American consultant in Düsseldorf to many large firms in the Ruhr, thinks this is the "next step." This next step is actually already under way.

Late in 1959, for instance, a subsidiary of the Ronson Corporation (cigarette lighters) opened a 28,000-square-foot plant in Germany at Deutz. This plant replaced one roughly one-fifth its size that had gone into production three years earlier. Production in the Ronson plant in 1959 was 100,000 lighters; 400,000 will be turned out in 1960. These lighters will be sold over most of Africa and the Far East. Furthermore, the company plans to produce at Deutz its new Windlight butane lighter for most of the world outside the United States.

Plant manager R. A. Forrest has been quoted as saying that "if all goes well" the plant will also be deluging the United States with its product to supplement output here. And this is only the beginning, for Ronson has acquired land to quadruple again the size of its factory.

Many other instances could be cited. Burroughs Corporation, makers of office machinery, in 1958 opened a factory in France at Rouen. Originally its production was to be only for Europe. But in October of 1959 the company announced that, because of competition from foreign firms in this country, it intended to import from Rouen to the United States.

American industry, once so insular in its outlook, so parochial in its approach, was moving with vengeance toward the internationalism that has always been such a marked characteristic of British businessmen. The backyard viewpoint was being swept away by the differential in manufacturing cost between the United States and abroad, by the huge potential of new markets coming into being abroad, by the realities of the new world economy that slid into being, almost unnoticed at first, in what financial writers like to call the "Fabulous Fifties."

Fabulous the Fifties may well have been, for they issued in for the United States and the American people a new age.

IX

The European Challenge, More Than Price

AMERICAN MANAGEMENT had always prided itself on its skill and know-how; but in 1953 and 1954 it began to become apparent that to a certain degree this had been less an achievement on our part than a result of weakness in others.

In most industries, American manufacturers traditionally had been able to compete with lower-wage foreign plant because, despite the wage differential, total costs had been kept competitive. American companies could afford a higher hourly rate because of superior manufacturing techniques. But after Korea we found that in many industries this was becoming less and less true, and that over-all costs were getting out of hand.

This was not true in all lines. It was not true, for instance, in coal, for reasons more than a little ironic.

Back in the 1930's and on up into World War II, John L. Lewis of the United Mine Workers had been the "sinister figure," the man who would wreck the American free enterprise system if given his way, and the terror of the station wagon set.

But Lewis realized that high wages and a high standard of living depended not only on heavy investment in ma-

chinery, but also on the abandonment of all restrictive practices which cut production per man-hour. Lewis was a mili-
tant labor leader, but in forcing his miners' wages up to the
highest in the country he never imposed featherbedding on
the coal industry. He was, as the expression went, ready to
trade jobs for high wages; and the wages he got in exchange
for his jobs could be high because his bargaining forced the
mines to mechanize to such an extent that today, despite its
wage level, United States coal is the cheapest in the world.
Coal from the Appalachian fields can be dug, shipped to
Norfolk, transhipped to Hamburg and then barged down the
Rhine to sell in Düsseldorf at a lower price than that mined
with relatively very low wages next door in the German
Ruhr.

It is an interesting commentary that the industry in
which we are most competitive in the world market happens
to be that which pays our highest hourly rate.

But in many industries, management bought industrial
peace by yielding on make-work and featherbedding issues,
and found itself later saddled with costs that prevented its
product from selling competitively. This was an issue in the
steel strike of 1959, on which, as of this writing, it looks as if
management yielded. The railroads, of course, are a prime
example. Featherbedding — the extra man in the cab of the
diesel — is said to cost the nation's carriers $400 million a
year, a sum which must be added to freight rates and therefore is reflected in the final price of American goods.

No longer in many lines could the wage differential be
covered by superior American techniques. American managerial ego was being deflated in areas other than costs,
however. As noted before, Philips, the electronics giant of
the Netherlands, is probably the world's most skilled mer-
chandiser — certainly a field we have always considered
particularly our own. Nor was superiority of design re-
stricted to the sewing machines and typewriters from Europe

which began to enter this country in large amount just before the Korean War.

The designers of Detroit had been caught napping, dreaming over their drawing boards of towering fins and masses of functionless chrome, cars that looked like a land submarine, even as the public taste was already shifting to the simpler lines and construction of the European car. Not until imports actually began to shake their fists in the face of the sales managers of Detroit did the magnates of Grosse Pointe abandon their stubborn insistence that what the American people wanted were ever more elaborate and bigger (never mind better) cars. The American consumer is the most researched creature on earth, but this was one boat that the researchers missed.

Superiority of European product is evident today in many lines: in glass, in tableware, in ceramics, in watches. The huge American motorcycle has become archaic, except for police officers. It was not price, but design, which gave the English bicycle manufacturers their first wedge into the American market. Actually the penetration that the British first achieved was against a domestic product that was lower-priced.

American publishers are having many books set and printed in Europe; not because it is cheaper, but because of quality and speed.

Nor is it only in consumers' goods that European design and often workmanship and engineering excel. Compagnie des Machines Bull, third largest manufacturer of computers in the world, is a leader in the field of smaller equipment — at least Bull itself believes this to the extent that it is planning to invest heavily in a plant in the United States. Nyerpic of Grenoble is one of the great companies of the world in such presently esoteric fields as tidal control and tidal power. The best towers to carry power transmission lines are not made in this country, but in Italy; and it was not cost differential but superior quality that led the New York Power Authority to give to Societa Anonima Elettrificazione of Milan the contract for its new Niagara Falls–Syracuse lines. American industry was by 1957 sitting up and blinking its eyes at the richness, variety and skill of European product development and research. As a matter of fact, industry did more than blink its eyes; it rushed abroad to avail itself of European skills.

Firms like Westinghouse, du Pont, Union Carbide and International Business Machines had been ahead of the rush and were already finding research help overseas. The newcomers, however, found facilities crowded, and research contracts hard to get. This has led some American research firms themselves to establish branches overseas which can tap European brains and experience for American clients. The famed Arthur D. Little, Inc., one of the world's leaders in the field, has a laboratory at Musselburgh, Scotland, and has had under consideration a branch in Switzerland to advise and guide American firms. Battelle Institute has laboratories in Geneva, Switzerland, and in Germany at Frankfurt. Battelle, however, is said to prefer to do business with European rather than American firms under the belief that European scientists might resent the American invasion to pick over their industrial secrets and research.

American steel companies are reported interested in European research in vacuum melting of ultrapure metals. Chemical companies have the Max Planck Society for the Advancement of Science in Mülheim, Germany, to thank for the first commercial process for manufacturing high-density polyethylene. A leader in polymer research is the University of Milan. Electronics manufacturers follow developments in Germany, Switzerland and Britain. Pharmaceutical companies watch steroid hormone research in Switzerland and France.

In short, by 1957 American firms were learning that two

basic assumptions traditional to industry in this country were no longer true, or at least were only half-truths:

(1) That it was the domestic market which really mattered, and that sales abroad were in a sense really only frosting for the domestic cake.

And (2) that we had been endowed from on high with a degree of managerial skill and know-how which made most of the rest of the world's industry, in comparison, just a little absurd.

American industry had been really challenged — on its ability to control costs and remain competitive, as well as on its superiority in design, merchandising and manufacturing techniques. Furthermore, industry could see ahead the day when the ECM would bring into being a degree of competition on the Continent which would almost inevitably still further sharpen European industrial skills, and a mass market which would give those skills such scope as had been enjoyed before only in the United States.

But industry saw something more. It saw that the basic structure of the relationship of the American economy and the world economy had changed: that we were becoming less and less a "have" nation, and more and more a "have-not nation"; that our industry today depended on large imports of crucial raw materials; that we would have to export in order to import and prosper; and that in many ways we now needed the rest of the world even more than the rest of the world needed us.

This lesson began to be spelled out in the intricacies of foreign exchange, balance of payments and the movement of gold. It was brought home finally and conclusively in the disappearance of something we thought of only a few years ago as a permanent fixture of the world economy — the so-called "dollar gap."

X

1957-59—The "Gold Years"

THE SWIFTNESS of economic change in the modern world is reflected in the following lead paragraphs of two articles which appeared just nine months apart:

"A slow, but steady, flow of gold into this country is raising concern among United States officials and those of other countries." — *U. S. News & World Report*, September 27, 1957.

"An outpouring of gold from this country — 1.2 billion dollars of it in just four months — is raising serious questions in the minds of many people." — *U. S. News & World Report*, June 27, 1958.

This change from an inflow of gold to an outflow of gold was not only dramatic in its suddenness, it was a reflection of a change in patterns of trade and foreign investment that was soon to treat very roughly indeed our preconceived notions on such matters as the balancing of our federal budget and the setting of monetary policy by the Federal Reserve.

The "concern" and "serious questions" of the two *U. S. News* articles were to become enlarged over the next fourteen months to the point where, in June and October of 1959, the two following leads could appear:

"Here are the key figures that are causing the American dollar to be viewed with such suspicion over much of the world . . ."

"The American dollar — once the proud symbol of a solidly solvent United States — today sells at a discount under the currencies of many other nations."

The views expressed in the two articles may have been somewhat alarmist, but at least the position of the dollar was enough in question even in December of 1958 to cause the brilliant and usually guarded Chairman of the Federal Reserve Board, William McChesney Martin, Jr., to state in a public speech in Chicago that on a recent trip to the Far East he had the "distressing experience" of finding among intelligent and perceptive men a "growing mistrust over the future of the American dollar."

Martin added that while he personally did not think such mistrust was justified, it was important for us to know why it existed. To the foreigner the dollar was the symbol of this country's strength; and a decline in its value would suggest to him a decline not only in the faith and credit of the United States, but also in moral force.

Two broad reasons were put forward as a reason for the mistrust. One was the feeling abroad that more and more the United States, through its inability to control its price level, would price itself out of world markets. The other was the huge deficit in the federal budget beginning to loom for the fiscal year of 1959, a deficit which finally came to $12.5 billion, the largest show of federal red ink during a peace year in our history.

Apparently in the banks of Calcutta and among exporters in such remote areas as Thailand and Hong Kong, the budget proposed by an American president and written by an American Congress was one of the main economic facts of life.

We had long been preaching to others the necessity of a stable currency, balanced budgets, a control of industrial prices. And others had heeded us, or proceeded on their own judgment and experience — Japan in 1948, Germany in 1949, Britain in 1946, Belgium in 1948 (France alone among industrial nations still had to make in 1957 the move back to whatever economic austerity was necessary to control inflation). Now these nations, themselves enjoying a high degree of prosperity and a rate of economic growth in some cases double that of our own, were expressing in their attitude toward the dollar the stricture: physician heal thyself.

The years of 1958 and 1959 were "the gold years," those in which for the first time in half a century the United States had to consider its position in gold. Since World War I our gold reserves had grown rapidly and with but minor interruptions: from $3.5 billion in 1922 to $24.5 billion in 1949.

From World War II until 1950, we had been wrestling with what used to be called the "dollar gap." This was a world shortage of dollars caused by the fact that only through the possession of dollars could the rest of the world command the goods that it needed to rebuild its war-torn economy and supply the plant and raw materials needed for economic growth. In 1950, however, we began to send abroad more dollars than the rest of the world spent in the United States — that is, the balance of payments turned against us — and this reversed the flow of gold into the United States.

The change gave no concern. Indeed, it was quite properly hailed as an indication of the success of the Marshall Plan and our whole postwar economic policy. An essential part of that policy had been to aid foreign nations in strengthening their currencies, which meant building up their balances of dollars and of gold. Besides, the deficit in our balance of payments remained small. Between 1951 and 1957, for instance, it touched $1.5 billion in only one year, and the average for the seven years was only $1.1 billion. Furthermore, the problem of the dollar gap — another word for an overfavorable balance of trade — would still have been with us if we had not been sending abroad so many dollars in foreign military and economic aid.

But then, in 1958, the balance of payments deficit suddenly yawned large . . . to $3.4 billion in 1958, and to some $4 billion in 1959. And in those years foreign nations, finding themselves earning more dollars than they had immediate need of, began to convert some of these dollars into gold — that is, they bought, or had put under their earmark in the Federal Reserve Bank in New York, considerable sums of gold.

The actual loss to us was not large, relatively. It amounted to $2.3 billion from 1957 to 1958, and roughly $1.7 billion in the following year. But the trend if continued obviously could breed dangers. No nation can continue to lose gold indefinitely. Nor could any nation continue indefinitely the adverse balance of payments position through which, of course, our loss of gold had come about.

Actually it is this balance-of-payments matter that is the real problem. It can and has been argued that it is not serious that we are sending abroad more dollars than the rest of the world is willing to spend in the United States. For instance, it is pointed out that $2.6 billion goes overseas every year in net payments on foreign aid, and that another sizable sum flows abroad in capital investment. But while we may succeed in getting other nations to join us in the industrial development of the underdeveloped nations (where almost all aid goes today), it is difficult to conceive of any material reduction in this outgo, if we are not simply to surrender large parts of Asia and Africa, and even Latin America, to communist doctrine. As for capital flowing abroad, that is in large part a reflection of the problem which constitutes the real core of the whole matter: costs and prices have risen in the United States relative to the rest of the world to the point where we are endangering our markets overseas, as well as actually surrendering to foreign manufacturers a part of our markets here. The current large outflow of capital is to build plant and other operations in lower-cost areas overseas.

Interestingly enough, the Europeans have been even more sharply aware than we of our danger in this direction, or at least have been more outspoken about it. In financial circles in London in the spring of 1959, it was being said that if the gold reserves of the United States were to be drawn down below $20 billion, steps would have to be taken — even if those steps involved a temporary suspension of all United States foreign aid!

Early in October of 1959, several Europeans were laying the problem squarely on the line. At the meeting of the Governors of the International Monetary Fund that month in Washington, Per Jacobsson, the fund's managing director, stated:

"The United States must have a balanced budget, must restrain credit and must curb costs and prices just as every other country must. It was by these means that the United Kingdom, Germany, Italy, and other countries have come to financial health, and that is what the United States is going to have to do, too."

At the same meeting, a leading French banker said: "You [the United States] profited handsomely from two world wars but, in the process, you forgot about costs, especially wage rates. Meanwhile, with your very generous help, Western Europe was rebuilt with modern machinery. This fact, plus a lower wage structure, has enabled Europe to become major competition for the United States. Even in France, in some lines we can outproduce you at lower costs. You are going to have to live with the new facts of life."

And an official of the new ECM warned: "At present, Western Europe is in such a strong competitive position that it is sucking gold and dollars out of the United States, just as the United States used to suck dollars out of Europe in the early postwar days . . . This is not a healthy situation."

The balance of payments represents, of course, the balance between the total flow of dollars in and out of a country for all purposes, including investment abroad and all foreign aid. But contained within that balance is what is perhaps a more significant figure, the balance of trade — that is, the flow in and out of dollars arising from commercial transactions, the buying and selling of goods and services (such as insurance).

This balance of trade is perhaps a more significant figure. The over-all payments position can be changed more easily — for instance, by cutting aid; or, as has been done in the past in many other nations, the forbidding of the exporting abroad of investment funds. But the balance of trade is the judgment of the law of supply and demand in the market place. It too is capable of influence, of course, by government action, through tariffs or quotas that restrict imports. But this is more difficult of accomplishment, and can be done, as a matter of fact, only by the erection of barriers, which constitute an admission of a loss of competitive position in world markets and which would involve a return to the protectionism that has written so much tragic economic history in the past.

And it was here, in the balance-of-trade position, that the trouble arose in 1958. As between 1957 and 1958, there was little change in either our total investment abroad or our payments under foreign aid. But our trade position deteriorated very rapidly. In 1957 we showed a favorable balance of $6.1 billion; in 1958, a favorable balance of $1.1 billion.

We still sold abroad more goods and services than we purchased abroad, but not enough more to offset the other factors making up our over-all payments position.

Perhaps it is an exaggeration to say — as it has been, frequently, in the last three years — that the United States was "pricing itself out of the world market." For one thing, 1957 was a year of heavy export from this country, in part due to oil shipments to cover Europe's need during the closing of the Suez Canal by Egyptian seizure that year, which cut down drastically on supplies from the Middle East. But there is unquestionably a substance of truth in the statement, and certainly it is glaringly true in many important lines.

This was the situation, then, that gave concern, and which found reflection in the piling up of what economists call foreign balances here — that is, dollars earned in trade by other nations for which they have no immediate need.

Such foreign balances have been increasing very rapidly of late — at the rate, actually, of some $4.5 billion annually. As of the end of 1959, foreign central banks held in this country dollar balances amounting to $9 billion. In addition, foreign private banks, corporations and individuals had in deposits and short-term investments (largely U. S. Treasury bills) another $10 billion. Potentially these balances — resulting from our unfavorable payments position — represent a claim on our gold stocks. The central banks abroad could convert their holdings of dollars into gold overnight, by simply ordering the gold put under earmark to their accounts by the New York Federal Reserve Bank. The private balances would first have to go through the intermediate step of being transferred to the central banks, but they also could be converted into gold in a short time.

Thus in that month, December, 1959, we had what in substance amounted to demand deposits against our gold reserves of some $19 billion, while our total gold stocks amounted to only $19.5 billion — of which $12 billion had by law to be held as a reserve against our currency in circulation. In other words, our so-called "free" gold was not sufficient to meet the potential claims that could be exercised against it.

It is easy to sound alarmist about this. Actually it is inconceivable that foreign nations would launch a "run on the dollar," which is what any mass conversion into gold would amount to. In the first place, such a move would wreck the whole economy of the free world, which, despite the relative loss of economic power by this country, still rests on the vastly productive plant and huge capital accumulations of the United States. For other nations to take any action that would substantially weaken the dollar would be very shortsighted of them indeed. The dollar's strength is actually the business of all free nations — as the British have been urging on everyone for two years.

Only some height of fiscal or monetary folly on our part could actually cause a flight from the dollar of such magnitude as to force us to the two means at our disposal for countering such an eventuality: an embargo on gold (which is like a bank suspending payment to depositors until, by liquidating loans, it can raise the money to satisfy depositor claims), or a devaluation of the dollar in terms of gold. The latter has long been talked of wishfully by the owners of gold mining stocks, for it would mean the raising of the price of gold from its present $35 an ounce. Its purpose, of course, would be to lessen the claims on gold held in foreign dollar balances by the amount of the rise in dollar price. But as such a move would be met instantly by a similar move throughout the rest of the world, and would therefore have in the end no net effect, the possibility has never been taken seriously by the European banks.

Actually the rapid build-up in foreign balances here, and the drawing down of our gold under foreign earmark, means only one thing: we can no longer act with complete freedom in economic policy. We are immeasurably the richest and strongest economic power in the world. But we are no longer so powerful, or the dollar so strong, that we can act without considering the reaction of others.

We must today set our economic policy and manage the fiscal and monetary affairs of our government under the realization that the central banks and others in Europe will be judging our actions — while at the same time holding in their power the means to register their reaction to our policies by moving their balances into gold, or repatriating them, thereby embarrassing us.

We are today like a bank which must conduct its affairs in a manner that will not shake the confidence of its depositors.

XI

The Lesson of Hard Money

WHILE THE DEFICIT in our balance of payments on foreign account has presented us with a serious problem, it is in fact another indication of the success of the Marshall Plan. To a much greater degree than the United States, other industrial nations of the world live by trade, and it was the increase in world trade that floated European and Japanese recovery. Such an increase would have been impossible without the building of gold and dollar reserves with which to finance transactions on foreign account, which meant, of course, some loss on the part of the United States. Thus the deficit in our balance of payments was healthy — up to a point. Without it the world economy today would be like a poker game, which slows down or has to be called off because one of the players (the United States) has won all the chips.

But in 1959, it became evident that we were losing our once big stack of chips too fast, and in the wrong way, and for the wrong reason. Ideally, we should have increased our volume of exports by a sufficiently large amount to cover our present export of dollars in foreign investment and foreign aid, or even in an amount which would have allowed us to increase such payments. This we have been unable to do, because of the loss of the competitive position of American goods in the world market, and in some industries in our domestic market.

It is interesting that this failure may well result in our hands being tied, in the use of our most potent anticyclical weapon. We have had three recessions since World War II — 1948, 1953, 1957-58. In each of these, the down-spiral which carries a relatively mild downturn in business into serious depression such as we have experienced in the past did not develop. There have been several reasons for this, and economists differ as to their relative importance; but in 1953 and 1957, a major stabilizing factor was the monetary policy of the Federal Reserve.

It has been the policy of the Federal Reserve system to "lean against the wind," to make money more plentiful, cheaper and easier to borrow when the economy began to turn downward . . . and to make money more expensive and difficult to borrow under reverse conditions, when a boom threatened and the economic wind carried the message of inflationary pressures. We have stimulated a weakening economy by making credit easy, which led business to borrow to invest. And we have held a checkrein on booms by slowing investment and spending by tightening credit.

The other countercyclical tool upon which we have relied in recent years is the handling of the federal budget. According to Keynesian, or the "new" economics — which are pretty well accepted in practice, although not in theory, by everyone today — the budget of a government should show a deficit when business contracts, and a surplus when times are booming. This is because budgetary deficits add to the money supply and increase debt (all increase in debt tends to be inflationary); while budgetary surpluses mean that the government is taking out of the economy more money than it is putting in, and decreasing debt. This is an over-simplification, for the process is complicated; but no economist today will seriously question the fact that the adjustment of a federal budget, as between surplus and deficit, is a strong countercyclical tool of equal or perhaps greater efficacy than monetary and fiscal policy.

But today could we use such countercyclical measures in the event of a downturn in the economy? Perhaps we could, but we cannot be sure. How would the holders of foreign balances here react to the sharp lowering of interest rates with which the Federal Reserve has countered nascent recessions in the past? The main reason these foreign balances have been left here is that higher interest rates have been obtainable here than abroad. If we were suddenly, for purely domestic reasons, to lower interest rates, we might well see a rapid withdrawal of balances — in other words, a repatriation of foreign funds back to Europe where interest rates might then be more attractive.

Furthermore, suppose that a cyclical downturn occurs and it becomes a matter of policy to show a deficit in the federal budget. What, under such circumstances, would be the reaction of the holders here of foreign funds who will allow their balances to remain only so long as they do not see the purchasing power of the dollar weakened? A budgetary deficit on the order of the $12.5 billion shown in fiscal 1959, which was in large part caused by the effort in Congress to check the recession of 1957-58, might well arouse fears as to our intention to maintain the value of the dollar and have even a more dramatic effect than the lowering of interest rates. There is, moreover, the very good chance that both steps might be taken simultaneously — or that we might want to take them simultaneously — in which case the foreign reaction would be compounded.

Such an eventuality might well see a run on the dollar, and on our gold, that would bring this country up short in a kind of crisis strange to us: a monetary crisis of the sort that Britain and other foreign nations have experienced often enough in recent years but which we have not seen in this country since the days shortly after the turn of the century when the elder J. P. Morgan bailed out the U. S. Treasury by arranging through the Rothschild interests in Europe the loan of a large sum of gold.

What this means, actually, is that we might face a situation in which we could counter a recession by orthodox means, only at the peril of finding ourselves in very serious trouble. This does not mean that we might not attempt to do so. The position in which we find ourselves is new to us, complicated, and subject to various interpretations as to cause and effect.

But the harsh truth is that in the event of another recession in this country, the economic facts of life might dictate at least a measure of deflation in order to protect our foreign position and our currency. This would involve the sort of belt-tightening with which American industry and labor are as yet unfamiliar; it would mean, in fact, a deliberate or voluntary dose of austerity. Would we take it? The question certainly raises serious doubts.

Remember, however, that the nations of Europe and Japan, which hold the foreign balances here and therefore, in a sense, will in their handling of those foreign balances be rendering a judgment on our economic policy, have in each instance themselves had to go through just such a period of austerity in order to stabilize their currencies. Indeed, it was we who urged it upon them in the past as a necessary step to rebuilding their economies after World War II. To be sure, we supported them with foreign aid at the time. But consistently over the past fifteen years we have preached the *sine qua non* of a sound currency and sound fiscal and monetary policy on others for economic prosperity and growth. We can therefore hardly expect others to be tolerant to the extent of jeopardizing their own best interests if we ourselves should depart from such a concept.

Furthermore, the nations of Europe as well as Japan are

much more sensitive to the whole inflation problem than
are we. Industry and labor here speak brave words on the
"dangers of inflation," but labor leaders are indifferent
to the inflationary effects of the wage increases they have
forced in recent years, and management in many industries
has been seemingly willing to go along as long as it could
pass on the added cost in higher prices.

Politicians also pay lip service, but stand ready to enact
inflationary legislation, either to reverse even a mild cor-
rective downturn, or because of the misconception that economic growth can be fostered by measures which act to increase the money supply.

There is, in fact, a whole school of economic thought in
this country that holds that "a little inflation" — say on the
order of a 2½ to 3 per cent rise annually in the price level —
is not too high a price to pay for the avoidance of even a
slight recession, and is at any rate necessary if we are to continue economic expansion. Still another school (the late
Sumner H. Slichter of Harvard was its best-known spokes-
man), while not condoning such "creeping" inflation, believes that it is unavoidable in a political entity such as the
United States where politicians are so directly subject to the
pressures of special groups and the labor unions are so well
organized and so politically strong.

Without going into the pros and cons of these arguments,
it might be noted that such points of view are not shared today in any country abroad.

The European — be he labor leader, or industrialist, or
politician — is in the matter of inflation very much the
burned child. All countries on the continent of Europe
have had it, as far as a depreciating currency is concerned.

Older people in Germany can remember when, after
World War II, their life savings became worthless, and the
housewife went shopping with a basket to carry the money
she would need, not in which to bring home her pur-
chases, which in those days were meager in any event.

Britain, trading all over the world and with the world's second most important currency, has no choice but to defend the pound sterling at almost any cost. The Swiss have always hewed to the hard-money line. Even the French and Italians, plagued by inflation, have turned to policies making the soundness of their currencies their prime objective . . . the French as a result of the sickening impact of seeing the franc sink from 49.5 to the dollar in November of 1946 to 493 to the dollar on January 1, 1959.

But what is of primary importance is that it has not been the experience of these nations in the postwar world that "a little inflation" leads to growth. They have found the opposite to be true: that is, that real economic growth can be built solidly into an economy only on the base and with the structural support of a sound currency.

This is a discovery — or, if you wish, a belief, but a belief upon which much of the world will act — of great significance. It could mean the end of "welfare state" economics. It is something which will certainly cut across present political lines in this country and sweep away the traditional issues of party politics. And it makes archaic much of the current thinking of the American press, which has yet to understand that a new world has been born in the expanding mills and factories of the postwar years and that politics no longer can be reported as a sort of game or contest between the Republican Elephant and the Democratic Donkey.

Politics today is an instrument to economic destiny.

XII

Stabilization in Britain and Germany

THE SETTING in order of their financial houses was undertaken by the various nations of Europe after World War II at different times and, to some degree, in different ways. But every country has been forced to the step, as a prerequisite to sustained recovery and economic solidity.

The first to move were the British. London is the banker to the whole sterling area, which includes much of the world outside the western hemisphere, and without a stable pound — without evidence that Britain stood ready to defend sterling — this role of banker could not be continued. Actually, more than the economic destinies of Britain were riding on the decision made in London in 1946.

The growers of jute in far-off Pakistan, the men who buy and sell the cacao of the African Gold Coast, the Australian beef trade, all had a stake in the willingness of the British people, wearied by war and war shortages, to continue the "austerity" of the war years. For only through such austerity, the holding down on consumption of goods at home, could Britain find the volume of exports necessary to pay for needed imports and at the same time build up gold and currency reserves through a favorable balance-of-payments position.

Rationing was continued. A heavy purchase tax was imposed on such items as might otherwise be drawn into the domestic market out of the export stream. The belt tightened by war was held to its tightness. This was a difficult period for Britain, and it lasted long. For years the economy walked a razor's edge. It was not until 1958 that the tide really turned and exports began to exceed imports by a comfortable margin.

The year 1957 marked the turning point. The British price level had at that time begun to edge upwards, and the trade unions were becoming restless. New and heavy wage demands seemed in the offing, when, suddenly, the Bank of England acted by raising its rate — the rate at which commercial banks could borrow — to 7 per cent.

This move had an electric effect on the financial world, for it served notice that Britain was prepared to defend sterling at almost any cost, whether political or economic, to the domestic economy. The message was as clear to the British unions as to everyone else. Britain would risk deflation, a recession at home, in order to maintain her foreign position.

The results of that handling of the "crisis" in September, 1957, were not entirely pleasant at the time for the British people, for in the next year unemployment rose by about 2 per cent. But prices were held relatively stable, and the case for sound money was carried.

In Germany the steps taken were entirely different. The German mark is not as important a currency in foreign trade as the British pound, and Germany was not a banker to any world area, although the need to export was equally real. However, the German people, who had suffered so fearfully under inflation after World War I, were willing to go to any length to strengthen and harden the mark for the job of reconstruction that lay ahead of them.

Actually the mark had first to be revalued — as was to

be the case with the French franc some years later — and this was done, not by the Germans themselves, but by the Allied occupation authorities. The step was taken in 1948: one new mark for ten old ones. Then came the surprise. Most of the world, including the Germans themselves, expected that the value of the new mark could be maintained only by continuing the strict rationing then in force in the West German Republic. But at Bonn was a remarkable man — a man destined to play a major role in the recovery of Europe, and who may yet turn out to be one of the architects of a new order of the whole West: the Minister of Finance, Ludwig Erhard.

Just three days after the announcement by the Allied authorities of the devaluation of the mark, Erhard went on the radio to address the German people. His words were dramatic. There would be no more controls over either prices or wages, no more rationing. The German economy was henceforth to be free. "We will turn the people and the money loose," he said. "They will make a strong Germany."

Erhard's edict aroused a storm of protest, both in Germany and abroad. It was pointed out to him that Germany, after all, had lost the war and in the process most of her industrial plant. How could the economy of the defeated be set free, when even victorious Britain and France still had to ration goods in their perilously balanced economies?

But Erhard stood by his guns — after a historic meeting with the then Military Governor, General Lucius Clay, who supported him. From now on, said Erhard, ". . . back to work and to rebuild. The mark is our only ration ticket."

For a while, it looked as if Erhard had made one of the most colossal monetary blunders of all time, for prices soared and German labor, infuriated by the hardship this entailed, demanded wage increases and a return to rationing. But Erhard kept insisting that prices would come down, would fall of their own weight in a free economy. He was right. By June of that year, the mark had returned to the value set by the Allied authorities, and there it remained, while German production soared. The mark was soon to rank with the Swiss franc as the soundest currency in Europe.

The story of Germany's economic achievement between 1947 and 1957 is so well known that it need only be mentioned in outline. Between 1948 and 1957, when the Common Market came into being, Germany's gross national product rose at an annual rate roughly twice that of the United States'. Unemployment vanished. By 1955, steel production had risen from the rubble of factories bombed out during the war to third place, exceeded only by that of the United States and the Soviet Union.

Between 1950 and 1957 alone the real wages of German workers rose by 60 per cent. In 1957 the furnaces of DE-MAG were turning out 13 per cent of the world's steel, and the technicians of Krupp were building such distant enterprises as a bridge in Columbia, a shipyard in Pakistan, and coal loading devices for the Chesapeake & Ohio Railroad on the docks of Newport News, Virginia.

The Bonn Government based its program for economic recovery on a drive for exports: heavy machinery, light machinery, chemicals, office equipment. German salesmen spread out over the world, Africa, Latin America, Asia, seeking to regain markets lost when the dark curtain of Hitler had fallen between them and the rest of the world, and to carve out new markets.

So successful were their efforts, and so large the volume of trade built up, that by 1955 German gold and dollar reserves had risen to $5.8 billion — roughly twice the reserves available to Britain in her function of banker to the whole sterling area.

Concurrently, Germany acted with quick economic imagination, dropping her own tariff barriers as fast as she could to allow the entry of foreign goods, and exporting capital herself on a relatively large scale. A technical assistance program of modest proportions was launched in 1957, and in that same year German industry itself invested abroad $380 million.

While the final turn came for Britain in 1958, it was 1952 which stamped the German recovery as lasting and real. In that year exports exceeded imports, and from then the margin continued to rise until in 1957, when the Treaty of Rome was signed, German sales abroad were running at $7.4 billion a year, exceeding imports by $690 million.

In those crucial preceding years, Germany had slashed her tariffs four times; no country in the world had ever lowered trade barriers so boldly. This had the twin effect of keeping domestic prices low, and at the same time allowing foreigners to sell goods in Germany and buy German goods in return. Seldom has the whole theory of free trade been as stoutly practiced, or found more dramatic justification.

It is interesting to compare the German rate of recovery and growth through those years with that of Britain. Between 1949 and 1956, investment averaged 18 per cent of gross national product in Britain, and 24 per cent in Germany. Measured in dollars, the actual figures show total gross investment for Britain of $39.4 billion; for Germany, $48.2 billion.

But the most significant figure of all is that of the wage cost per unit of output, which rose, 1949-56, by 29 per cent in Britain and by only 6 per cent in Germany. There were several reasons for this difference. Trade unions in Germany were in those years as dedicated as industry or the government to maintaining a favorable price position in world markets. In Britain the unions were more aggressive in their demands for wage increases. Another factor was the steady flow of workers from East Germany, which acted to some degree to stabilize wages.

But it was results that mattered. By 1959 Germany could claim 9.2 per cent of the world export market, just about her share before Hitler's rise to power. In regaining their lost ground, German exporters trod, of course, on many toes, but on none more heavily than those of their great traditional trade rivals, the British.

In Canada, a British Commonwealth market, German sales rose from $30 million to $104 million between 1953 and 1958. In the latter year, Germany had to a large extent supplanted Britain's prewar position in the metal and machinery industry of the Argentine, and was pressing the British hard in their once almost closed market of Portugal. In that same year German exports to Red China stood at $162 million, and a German consortium was given the contract to build a $525-million steel mill in India.

American firms too were feeling the weight of German competition. Mercedes was pressing Kaiser hard in Argentina; German chemicals and German drugs, German tractors and German machinery were cutting into markets, throughout the world that, since the war, American manufacturers had begun to think of as exclusively theirs.

The German recovery was soon to reach a sort of plateau; by the end of 1958 it had, for the moment at least, run somewhat low on steam and the spotlight of economic Europe was turning to more recent comers, Italy and France. But the German achievements in the postwar years remain as a historic example of what could be accomplished by a nation willing to work, wise in its grasp of economic essentials, and able to plan and act with economic imagination.

It is, in fact, because of the policies followed by Germany in those years that the European Common Market could emerge from concept into actuality in 1957. Germany's willingness to lower tariff barriers, Germany's eagerness to export capital, Germany's vision in seeing that her own economic future was tied up with the future of all Europe,

Germany's willingness, as a matter of fact, to underwrite to a certain extent the deficit of France in foreign account after the ending of U. S. aid, were all factors which combined to create in large part the base upon which today the "new" Europe rests.

A hideous political distortion in Germany had plunged the world into World War II. But it was German economic vision which, on top of U. S. aid, made possible the rebuilding from the ruins of that conflict. Such, sometimes, are the ironies of history.

XIII

The "Hard" Franc Ushers In a New Decade

Throughout the postwar years, the nations of Europe were moving slowly, one by one, toward a new "economic conservatism," the core of which was sound money. Gradually their currencies were hardening, as against the dollar. Industry in Europe is not as sensitive as in the United States to government ownership of certain industries; in Italy, France, even Germany, many large enterprises are government-owned — aircraft, steel, automobile, natural gas, oil production and refining as well, of course, as utilities and railroads — but private enterprise sees in this no gathering cloud of socialism. Even the stoutest conservatives are reconciled to a mixed economy in which the state controls at least some industry. And only when the government-operated industry begins to play very rough competitively — as, for instance, Enrico Mattei's ENI gas and oil combine in Italy — are there rumbles from such sectors of the private economy as may be hurt.

The Europeans have also gone further along the path of the welfare state than have we — that is, in such matters as social security and benefits and job security (payments made by the employer under all social security programs may amount to over 50 per cent of an employee's wage check).

But in fiscal and monetary policy, the trend has been in the opposite direction and Europe today is far to the Right.

What this means, actually, is that sound money is regarded as an economic objective of equal, if not even greater importance than the maintaining of full employment. This is not true of the United States, where the Act of 1946 makes full employment a mandatory objective of government policy but makes no mention of the protection of the currency.

To be sure, the new monetary conservatism of Europe has not been put to the test of a serious recession; and in that eventuality, with really serious unemployment, we might well see some profound changes. But such changes would probably not carry Europe back to the "soft currency" practices of the recent past. The result would more likely be of a radical political nature: that is, a political upheaval which would bring into power groups which would socialize much of industry along Marxist or semi-Marxist lines, while at the same time maintaining the integrity of national currencies.

A socialist or semisocialist state following the most conservative and orthodox monetary policy is not a contradiction per se, as witness the Soviet Union, which is punctilious in settling its foreign accounts in gold that is both beautifully packaged and always just a little underassayed — "a joy to handle," say the European banks.

In short, while nothing is certain in economics, all the evidence points to the nations of Europe continuing under almost any conceivable circumstances to defend their currencies by any means possible whenever it shall become necessary. And the great lesson that the United States will have to learn is that under its present balance-of-payments position, it will have to do likewise . . . or see the dollar steadily weaken as against the other currencies of the West.

The last nation in Europe to come to orthodox or conservative monetary management was France. Italy cut the root of the savage war and immediate postwar inflation in late 1947 by certain monetary measures. Wholesale and export prices now are actually below the average for the year 1948. Although the cost-of-living index rose subsequently, owing to the relaxing of controlled rents (in order to stimulate building), and rises in certain food products and utility rates, the rise was less over the 1947-58 period than in the United States. Belgium stabilized in 1948; also the Dutch, who had to move quickly with a belt-tightening operation in 1954 when inflation again threatened their monetary dikes. But France appeared as late as May, 1957, to be incorrigibly committed to soft money, her entire economic future hostage to a political instability that left her powerless to defend the franc.

When in that month Socialist Premier Guy Mollet was tumbled from power by the National Assembly, it appeared that the nation had come to the end of the line.

Economists of the Commissariat au Plan (roughly comparable to our Council of Economic Advisors) were privately predicting catastrophe. Despite great natural wealth, and plenty of liquid wealth in the hands of her people, France was being drained by an unfavorable trade balance — a danger hitherto held at arm's length by West Germany and the United States. She was losing gold rapidly. Her domestic budget was far out of balance. Most of her industry, long used to the twin crutch of cartels at home and high tariffs against imports from abroad, did not appear able to compete with that of either Germany or Italy, as it would shortly have to do if the European Common Market, just organized, was to have any reality. Algeria seemed to be bleeding her to a slow economic death. And throughout Europe it was being said that German industry seemed set to accomplish by economic means that which the Wehrmacht twice within thirty years had attempted, and failed: to "take over" France.

In November of 1957, for instance, *U. S. News & World*

Report carried an article on France with the following head: "France: Now the Real Showdown — Bankruptcy, Collapse Threaten the Key U. S. Ally."

And again on April 25, 1958, from the same magazine: "Blow-up in France: New Worry for U. S."

That was a crucial year for the European Common Market, indeed for the whole future of the West; for the Market and the entire cause of European unity hung in the balance. Without France, Europe would have been turned back to the segmented, national economies of the past. A bankrupt France would have pulled half of Europe down with her. Many in Europe as well as the United States must then have wondered as to the wisdom of supporting France in the postwar years. There was the aid from the United States: $2.5 billion in loans; military aid to French forces in Europe, $3.9 billion; military aid for the Indo-China war, $1.6 billion; economic aid and defense support, $3.1 billion. West Germany too had been generous with credits and support in more recent years. Was all this support to go down the drain?

General Charles de Gaulle answered that question in 1958, when he came to power on the shoulders of the battle-hardened paratroopers in Algeria; and in that event and the fall of the Fourth Republic was written an economic story of dramatic impact that changed the history of our times.

De Gaulle and his Finance Minister Antoine Pinay moved quickly.

France had been going through a frantic boom in industrial investment, caused by an inflation which in its turn was the result of huge deficits in the national budget. One of Pinay's first moves was to cut the deficit in half. Credit restrictions were imposed, a limit set on price increases, and plans made to devalue and then stabilize the franc. So quickly did events move in 1958 that the *Journal of Commerce* in October of that year, just a few months after de Gaulle took power, wrote: "A sort of industrial recession is in the air in France today." That certainly was no exaggeration. An economy which, inflation-fed, had been growing at the rate of 6 to 10 per cent in recent years, had dropped back to an annual rate of expansion of just 1.5 per cent.

The devaluation of the franc followed quickly. On December 26, all financial markets were closed because of "a decision which will be taken by the Government." The next day came the announcement: the franc was to be devalued by an amount which, measured in dollars, brought it from 420 to the dollar to 493.7. And with that action, France entered upon her version of that "austerity" which all other nations in Europe had gone through at one period in the postwar years in order to stabilize their currencies and hold inflation in check.

This program included the raising of taxes, the reduction of social security, the reduction of state subsidies for such basic consumer items as bread, wine, tobacco, coal, utilities and transportation. For the French economy these measures meant monetary stability. For French industry the devaluation of the franc meant a stronger price position in the export market. But for the French people the events of that year meant an acceptance of a lower real income — the holding down of wages at a time when domestic, in contrast to export, prices were bound to rise.

The great question that year, of course, was: How would the French people react politically? Could de Gaulle hold them to the path of orthodox finance being instituted by Pinay?

France had been the great question mark hanging over the Common Market, for France more than any other had stood to be hurt. The drafters of the Treaty of Rome had realized this, and had been careful to write into the Treaty certain clauses designed to ease France's way into the new

economic community. These were clauses that provided
for postponements of the scheduled tariff cuts, if they imposed too great a hardship, and allowed the postponement
of the dropping of quotas if the hurt was too severe. They
were clauses, in fact, which made as easy as possible what
everyone knew to be the great uncertainty hanging over
European economic unity: could the industry of France
come out of the hothouse of protectionism and domestic
cartels to survive in the harsh, driving, competitive Europe
that the Market would usher in?

The first of those tariff cuts under the Rome Treaty went
into effect on January 1, 1959. France invoked none of the
"escape" clauses, and went along. De Gaulle held the people with him, and to Pinay's austerity program. By April of
1959, the situation was such that the *Wall Street Journal*
could state: "For the first time in more than ten years
France's foreign credits are greater than her 'debits' . . .
credits of $1.4 billion, foreign debt of $1.2 billion . . . with
$590 million in gold held in the Bank of France."

By the following month, May, France's gold reserves were
up $1 billion, and the French economy was universally re-
garded as sound, as "firm."

In June, it was suddenly realized that France, because
of the devalued and then stabilized franc, was strongly competitive with both West Germany and Britain, her two
trade rivals in Europe. The Bank of France had cut the interest or discount rate twice, from 4½ to 4¼ to 4 per cent.
For the first time in living memory, American tourists visiting Europe for the summer had the eye-opening experience
of having to pay a premium over the official rate when they
turned their U. S. dollars into French francs. So strong had
the French economy become that one writer on European
economic affairs stated that it could now actually stand the
drain of the Algerian War, whereas only six months before
this struggle had seemed to threaten French economic
collapse.

It is interesting that within a year and a half of French stability under de Gaulle, the entire viewpoint of the world toward France had changed. Actually, the French economy had been far stronger intrinsically than most observers — at least most observers in the United States — had realized. Its strength had been hidden by political instability, by consistent inflation and the consequent flight of large amounts of private capital abroad, by its two costly wars in Indo-China and Algeria, and by the peculiar naïveté of Americans, who for some reason have always taken a rather patronizing attitude toward French business.

In reality French industry has always been enormously skilled in certain lines. Furthermore — a fact not generally realized — destruction of French industrial plant during the German offensive of 1945 was as great as that in Germany. Much plant has therefore been rebuilt, and along the most modern and efficient lines. France, furthermore, has great agricultural resources and is the only country in Europe able to feed itself in a normal year.

Then too France had discovered an Aladdin's lamp to new wealth in her new oil and gas discoveries — first at Lacq, near the Spanish border, and then later in fabulous amount in the Sahara, where today lie petroleum riches exceeded only by those of the Middle East.

On December 6, 1959, the spigot was turned which sent the first oil flowing toward Europe from the Saharan fields. This was through a 412-mile, $80-million pipeline from the wells at Hassi Messaoud to the Mediterranean port of Bougie. A second line, now under construction, will cross Tunisia to another field at Edjele; it is scheduled for opening in 1961. Still other pipeline routes are being surveyed, both for gas and oil, one from Africa which would cross the Mediterranean to feed into Europe at some point on the Spanish coast.

All told, France has sunk about $800 million into her Saharan oil venture, and with sound justification. While crude is in oversupply throughout the world, most of Europe must buy all but a small amount of its supplies from either British or American companies, and pay for them with dollars or sterling. And the foreign exchange to pay for these imports of petroleum must, of course, be earned — earned, that is, by the export of other European products to raise this foreign exchange. Much of France's recent foreign deficit was caused by the $490 million she has been forced to pay annually for petroleum products in either dollars or British pounds.

Oil from the Sahara will change this, not only for France but for all Common Market nations, which will be able in the future to buy Saharan oil for European currencies. This will be an ever-increasing boon to Europe, as the Continent is now rapidly turning for fuel from high-cost coal to oil.

As for France itself, the Saharan venture has fired the imagination of the whole nation. (One of the reasons for the stubbornness of French public opinion on the Algerian question is the fear that an independent and hostile Algeria might attempt to shut France off from her new sources of crude.) Oil is energy, and energy is wealth in modern industrial society. French officials believe that the Sahara will make France the world's ninth petroleum producer by the close of 1961, and the fifth by 1964, when she will be exceeded only by the United States, the Middle East, Venezuela and the Soviet Union. Nor is oil the only wealth of the Sahara; beneath the desert are many valuable minerals, including large deposits of iron and uranium ores.

Many other facets of strength in the French economy have been overlooked. Metropolitan France and the French community are rich in bauxite (aluminum) ore, iron, coal, uranium, natural gas and water power. France has a superb network of railroads. In her main export lines — certain kinds of electrical equipment, computers, special machinery, besides luxury goods — her competitive position is very strong. Most significant of all, perhaps, is the not always appreciated fact that the French workman is probably the best in Europe. There are those who deny this — who would give the blue ribbon for productivity to the German, or even the Italian. But in recent years French industrial productivity — the output per individual working hour — has been higher in France than in either Germany or Italy. Behind the screen of inflation and political instability, the French gross national product increased in the decade ending in 1959 by 55 per cent.

In 1958, the rate of industrial output in France passed that of West Germany in percentage growth, as against 1953; and projections published in *Business Week* in June, 1959, saw total French output as exceeding that of either Britain or Germany in gross amount by 1970. In other words, in another ten years France may well be Europe's leading economic power.

French computers today rank first in Europe. French aluminum and steel are the world's lowest priced. French techniques have set a new standard in making coke for the steel industry. France is second only to Britain in the export of aircraft — the twin-jet transport made by Sud Aviation and called the Caravelle is outstanding for flights up to 900 miles, and is being bought by airlines in many countries, including the United States. French automobiles are competitive everywhere. In fact, so strong is the French economy today that in mid-October, 1959, the British economic commentator Colin Brogan wrote in the *Sunday Graphic*: ". . . believe it or not, the immense economic progress of France outstrips even the widely advertised advance made by West Germany." He then added that "it was more than a probability" that France was going to have the highest per capita wealth in the world.

In that same October, France canceled a $200-million stand-by credit with a group of twenty-one commercial banks in the United States, comanaged by the Chase Manhattan and First National City of New York. The credit had been arranged the previous January, in case the franc should need stabilizing after the devaluation in December. But it was not needed. French gold and foreign currency reserves reached close to a record $2 billion in that same month.

There are always political uncertainties in France. We saw, in February of 1960, the crisis in Algeria, when it looked for a week as if de Gaulle might be toppled from power by those same French troops in North Africa whose support had lifted him to power two and a half years earlier. At the same time there was the resignation of Antoine Pinay, Finance Minister and architect of France's new monetary stability. French politics are always difficult for a foreigner to understand, with individual motives often obscure, and maneuvering behind the scenes which seems frequently only a maze of bewildering contradictions.

But if we assume that de Gaulle will remain, or that his eventual successor will continue in essence the de Gaulle monetary policies, France's economic power and influence in the coming decade will mount and reach far and wide.

In the first place, a hard franc will bring enormous sums of capital back to France. The French are individually the richest people in Europe, but a steady depreciation of the currency has sent large amounts of capital into hiding: into gold coins, in the case of the peasantry and shopkeepers (an estimated $2 billion worth) . . . and on the part of the more knowledgeable, into foreign investments, much in common stocks in the United States. No figures are available; but the best-informed guesses place the sum total of all capital fugitive from a depreciated franc at $11 billion.

This capital is already beginning to drift back. As a matter of fact, the repatriation of French and other European investments in the United States was generally believed to have played a role in the weakness in January, 1960, in the

New York Stock Market. As this repatriation continues, it will make available to French industry at home, as well as French associated economies overseas, a very large amount of fresh capital.

But a "sound money" France will speak with a voice that every American too will hear. In previous chapters we have noted the significance of the large short-term balances being held in the United States by foreign nations. We have seen, furthermore, that these balances may be remaining here in part at least because of our current high interest rates, and that in any event they might well be drawn down quickly into gold if or when their holders abroad began to suspect that we were either unwilling or politically unable to defend the value of the dollar as against European currencies.

France is one of the holders of these important sensitive foreign balances — well over $1 billion as of the first of 1960. And the sudden conversion of these French holdings could start a drift away (if not, actually, a run from) the dollar that could have very serious repercussions indeed. Furthermore, a France dedicated to a hard franc might well be quicker to move in any possible conversion of foreign dollar balances than would most other European nations.

In such matters the French are prone to act quickly. They take a somewhat more limited or less imaginative view than, for instance, the British or the Germans, and are therefore apt to act more readily on what seems to them their immediate self-interest. It was France which forced Britain off gold in 1931, and by just this means — the withdrawal of French balances held at that time in London. Furthermore, this was done deliberately by the Bank of France. It is an admitted fact that France then tried to use her holdings of large sterling balances as a club over Britain in order to influence British foreign policy.

Is it stretching things a little far to see a French government saying in effect to Washington that the leaving of balances in the United States would be contingent upon, for instance, U. S. support for French policy in Algeria in the United Nations? Perhaps. But perhaps not. The objectives of nations are pursued relentlessly in a world where the economic well-being of a people is at once the issue and the goal of most foreign policy. There is no "playing the gentleman" in the realities of the market place, and ethics does not enter the judgment of the banking centers of the industrial powers.

France — a France determined at all costs to rise to a position on a par with Britain in both military and economic power — might very well attempt in the United States what she attempted almost thirty years ago in London: to exert political pressure through her possession of large dollar balances.

This whole situation, as a matter of fact, has about it an almost cosmic cast of irony. For a generation, Americans have regarded the franc as "soft," a currency not to be taken quite seriously. At the same time we have held a picture of France as a playground, a country to visit as tourists, a producer of wines, perfumes, fashions and pleasure.

Now suddenly looms a new France that might someday say to us that it is not content to leave its capital here because it mistrusts the dollar . . . a France that could conceivably attempt political pressure through the threat of its handling of its dollar balances . . . a France that through leadership of the European Common Market may yet impose on the United States new realities which will touch not only our foreign economic policy, but the earnings of American corporations and, conceivably, even the wages of American labor.

This is surely one of the most dramatic stories of modern times. It illustrates and brings home in clearest terms the message which no one has put more succinctly than Peter F.

Drucker, one of the most astute business thinkers in the United States and the author of *Landmarks of Tomorrow*. In the May-June, 1959, issue of the *Harvard Business Review*, the magazine published by the Harvard School of Business Administration, Mr. Drucker wrote:

> *American public and business policies reflect some basic assumptions regarding our position in the world economy. With some oversimplification, these assumptions can be summarized in the following four statements:*
>
> *(1) the domestic market is the most important market for the American economy; performance in it is a full measure both of the American business and of the American economy.*
>
> *(2) American superiority in productivity and in technological and managerial knowledge is "normal" (some people may even say "God given," I suspect).*
>
> *(3) the "dollar gap" is a permanent fixture of the international economy; foreign countries want as many American goods as they can get — and they want much more from us than we shall ever want from them.*
>
> *(4) altogether the world economy needs us more than we need it.*
>
> *These assumptions are widely considered — by laymen as well as businessmen, labor leaders, and Congressmen — to be self-evident truths if not inexorable laws of nature. I believe, however, that in fact they not only are dangerously taken for granted but echo much of the complacency with which Edwardian England viewed its place in the world (to the sorrow of Britons ever since World War I). The assumptions are also at best half-truths — and rapidly becoming less true all the time. An almost opposite set of assumptions would, I submit, be far closer to the truth.*

More than a decade drew to a close in the months following Drucker's article. He had put his finger on one of the turning points in economic history, of this country but also of the world. American industry, American labor, American politicians at the beginning of 1960, whether they were aware of it or not, faced an era in which profound adjustments would have to be made in their thinking, and in policy. The world had emerged into a new and harsher economic reality. The philosophy of the New-Fair Deal had become meaningless. Before us was opening a period of enormous opportunity in which new concepts would have to be formed and our understanding of the modern world deepened. The decade ahead will be a demanding one, for along with its opportunities it presents problems and it is not without dangers — specifically the great over-all danger of our allowing our domestic economic policy to be formed by concepts no longer valid, our ideas left hostage to an era already passed.

XIV

Transistors and Textiles from Across the Pacific

THE ELECTRONICS industry is new. Its product is dramatic. The missiles that may in the not too distant future voyage into space, the giant computers whose silently moving tapes are taking over much of the clerical work of modern industry, controls in plant and factory that guide the new assembly lines, the entertainment field and, above all, modern weapons are dependent on the plants which have sprung up only within the last five or six years to manufacture the components of electronics, while ahead lie new frontiers not even identified as yet, far less conquered.

The surge of electronics manufacture in the United States in the late 1950's meant much to this country, both to certain areas such as California and Massachusetts in the growth it provided, and to the nation as a whole, which found in the new industry a source of national pride and an indication of industrial leadership.

But as early as 1957, the first clouds began to gather. In that year Japanese electronics manufacturers sold in the United States 641,000 small radio sets, mostly transistorized portables. In the following year Japanese exports to the United States soared to 2,500,000 sets. In the first nine months of 1959, the figure had reached 3,900,000 and estimates were that in the final months of that year the Japanese were taking roughly half of the American market in the four-or-more transistor radios.

Furthermore, in the first nine months of 1959 Japanese sales of loose transistors for use both in radios and in other electronic products rose from 10,600 in all of 1958 to 1,828,000.

This was one of the swiftest pre-emptions of a new market by import ever seen by industry. It was, moreover, apparently not to stop at that point.

Late in 1959, Japan's Sony Corporation unveiled an 8-inch, 23-transistor portable television set. This TV, about the size of a shoe box, weighs only thirteen pounds. It operates on a built-in, rechargeable storage battery, or it can use ordinary house current. It is scheduled for the Japanese market in April of 1960 and will be introduced to the American market before the end of the year, priced perhaps as low as $150. A similar set by Tokyo Shibaura is planned for the export market a few months later.

But the Japanese industry has still further plans for the rich market suddenly uncovered in the United States in this new industry. These include larger radios using up to sixteen transistors for regular FM and short-wave reception, midget tape recorders, portable phonographs, hearing aids and transistorized clocks. Matsushita of Osaka is making a midget portable radio which will fit in a shirt pocket, for sale by U. S. jewelers who handle the Bulova watch.

To this situation the industry in the United States reacted in two ways. In the fall of 1959, the Electronics Industry Association petitioned the Office of Civil and Defense Mobilization to investigate and take "appropriate action." The E.I.A. pointed out that imported transistors were selling at 80 cents or less, as against an average price in the United States of $1.35. Such a situation, if unchecked, would endanger the national security, the E.I.A. argued, as transistors were vital to modern military equipment and the price differential would soon throttle American research and development. In other words, the defense function of the electronics industry would be jeopardized by the loss of so much of its civilian market.

American firms were not content to wait on a ruling from the OCDM, however. Here was competition similar to that being met in the world market from producers in Europe — although not in the same field; European manufacturers find no local market for low-priced radios and have no relish for meeting Japanese competition in this field in the United States.

But the situation was different. An American manufacturer running into competitive trouble with his European rivals could "join them" by building manufacturing facilities abroad to take advantage of European wage rates. But this, generally speaking, was not possible in Japan. The Japanese, while living by trade, are strongly nationalistic in domestic economic policy; and no red carpet rolls out from Tokyo toward American firms interested in direct investment there. Singer is in Japan with a subsidiary, also Dow Chemical and Minneapolis-Honeywell. Most American firms, however, find their entry into Japan blocked by business firms there who can generate no enthusiasm for competing with American manufacturing techniques paying Japanese wage rates.

Yet the lure of these wage rates is strong for American industry which must meet Japanese competition in its own domestic market. In some small shops in Tokyo, workers as young as fifteen work at benches to turn out midget radios for as little as $3.85 to $10 a week, depending on age and job, and enjoy almost no fringe benefits. On the other hand big firms like Matsushita of Osaka, with 20,000 employees, pay from $4.50 to $29 a week. On top of this, such companies give large semiannual bonuses, provide medical benefits, pensions, practically free company housing, cut-rate

cafeterias and company stores. Actually such large companies provide the social security drawn from government in
most other countries. This may increase labor costs over
wage rates by as much as 130 per cent. Matsushita is said
to have an actual average wage cost of $25.70 per worker.

But even this figure is very low by United States standards, where average weekly earnings in electrical machinery
stood at $90.72 at the close of 1959. And to this differential
American firms reacted by either contracting to have parts
made in Japan for assembly into finished product here, or
arranging to have the end product made entirely in Japan
to their specification. Some firms employ both methods.

Motorola, for instance, had been buying parts in Japan
for some time for its U. S.-assembled radios and phonographs. It is now introducing an entirely Japanese-made
small portable, fabricated by Tokyo Shibaura Electric, for
sale in the United States.

Trav-ler Radio of Chicago, after struggling to compete
with its domestic product, threw in the sponge in 1959 and
arranged for Japanese-made parts to be assembled in Chi-·
cago. Emerson is selling under its Jefferson-Trazis trade-
mark around 20,000 radios a month made for it by Standard
Radio of Tokyo. RCA is using Sanyo Electric of Osaka as a
fabricator for the non-North American market of its Victor
brand.

There is, of course, nothing new in Japanese competition;
Made in Japan have been fighting words for several American industries for a number of years. But the problem is different today. Formerly the Japanese label was synonymous
with cheapness, usually an imitation of some foreign product. But postwar Japan is bending every effort to upgrade
its industrial products to match those of Europe and the
United States.

The large Tokyo department store, Takashimaya, opened
a store in New York on Fifth Avenue in October of 1958.

The purpose was twofold: to introduce U. S. customers to quality Japanese goods, and to aid the West and the East to meet on trading terms that would not arouse public opinion against Japanese imports into the United States. The New York store carries dolls ranging up to $120 each, rare antiques, lacquerware, fine china, screens selling for as much as $1200, $3000 kimonos, wooden chests, lacquer tables, fabrics up to $15 a yard. Through such merchandise, the Japanese hope to avoid the so-called "voluntary" agreements to limit exports to which they were forced on cotton goods destined for the United States.

The first of these "voluntary" quotas was arranged when Japanese Prime Minister Nobusuke Kishi visited Washington in the spring of 1957. The previous year had seen Japan's total volume of exports soar to $2.5 billion, a fivefold increase over 1949. Of these exports, 22 per cent, almost half of which were textiles — $200 million worth — came to the United States.

This entry of textiles aroused the American industry, which appealed to the Tariff Commission as early as 1955. But the Commission had refused to take action. It denied the industry's assertion that U. S. mills were being seriously threatened by imports from the Far East, saying: "Textile manufacturers in Japan do not have an across the board competitive advantage."

These were the Commission's points, made in a ruling handed down in May of 1956:

An exceedingly small part of domestic consumption of cotton manufacture is supplied by imports; and the Japanese get only a part of this . . .

Many parts of the United States textile industry can stand up to the competition of imports . . .

In the preceding year Japan had purchased 5 times as much raw cotton in the United States as was contained in the textiles it exported to the United States.

As proof that much of our textile industry was competitive, the Commission cited the sale of American textiles in the world market where it had to compete without preferential treatment . . . the fact that our exports of textiles exceeded our imports by a wide margin . . . and that we had actually in the preceding year sold $350,000 worth of textiles in Japan.

Turning from the Tariff Commission, the textile industry began to speak forcibly to representatives of the mill states in Congress. The result was a quick coming to heel by the Japanese, who saw the danger of tariff walls being thrown up in their face. The result was the so-called voluntary agreement, under which Japan agreed to limit her exports of cotton to this country to 235 million square yards annually over a period of five years. The total included both yard goods and made-up products, and was expected to remain the same over the life of the agreement, although individual product quotas could be negotiated. The net effect of this arrangement was to freeze imports at some 10 to 15 per cent below the 1956 level, and it is worth noting in passing that this meant that Japan could sell us no more than some 197 million yards annually. But the final quota figure was, as stated by *Business Week* at the time, "in proportion to the political pressure."

One may wonder just how much the American industry had been crying wolf, and how much it really had been hurt. Total textile production in this country was at that time on the order of $13.5 billion, against which the $200 million imported from Japan does not seem like much of a loss of market. But more than the volume, it was the price effect of the Japanese imports that the domestic industry here was concerned over; and it was probably true that the imports did tend to depress the prices at which mills could move goods here.

Small as was the volume of imports measured against U. S.

production the results of the quota agreement were unfortunate for Japan, which ran into a trade deficit of roughly
$400 million in the first six months of the following year.
In an effort to correct this deficit, Japan sliced her imports
drastically, reducing by 25 per cent her imports of American cotton, for instance, as well as many industrial products
of American make.

This brought home to American industry the importance
of Japan as a customer. In 1956, Japan had bought from
the United States $900 million worth of goods, which placed
her almost equal with Britain as our second-best customer
(Canada is first). Furthermore, ironically enough, Japan
was at the time buying from us almost twice as much as she
was selling us. All economic logic pointed to encouraging
Japanese sales in this country in order to increase further
U. S. sales in Japan. But logic had nothing to do with the
laws passed in some of the Southern states requiring a store
selling Japanese goods to display a sign in its windows advertising that fact.

As of this writing, the OCDM has not ruled on the peti-
tion of the Electronics Industry Association to investigate
and take "appropriate action" against Japanese electronic
exports to this country. Probably it will never have to. In
the matter of trade with the United States Japan has a sensitive nerve, and what we shall probably see is another "voluntary" quota agreement.

XV

The "Voluntary" Quota

EUROPEAN AND Japanese industry keeps an ever watchful eye on American reaction to the actuality or threat of rising imports. It is said, for instance, that there is an informal association of German and French producers which controls the imports of its membership into the United States. The purpose of this is to avoid pressing their advantage too hard and thereby forcing the United States to take countermeasures. This may be somewhat of an exaggeration; but it is certainly true that industries abroad which aim at the market in the United States keep a very close finger on the political and economic pulse of public and business opinion in this country.

In Japan, for instance, is the so-called JETRO, the Japanese External Trade Recovery Organization. JETRO is continually pushing Japanese industry to upgrade the quality of its export products, or to aim for the higher-priced foreign market. This pressure has two purposes besides a natural desire, as a matter of national pride, to end the association in the foreign mind between the label *Made in Japan* and cheap merchandise. In the first place, it broadens the export base by opening new markets. Of even greater importance is the fact that the higher-priced imports into a country do not as a rule arouse the demand for protection to the same degree as do imports of low-priced products.

Cheap Japanese chinaware, for instance, has always aroused feelings of violence in producers in the United States, and the Japanese have bowed to this trade fact of life with a voluntary agreement in principle similar to that in textiles. Under this agreement, Japan has forbidden entirely the export of 93-piece dinner sets or their equivalent at a price lower than $16 f.o.b. Japan. And sets priced between $16 and $17 are limited by a quota for export to the United States of 10,000 annually.

But it has not been found necessary to cover the higher-priced merchandise with the quota. As a result, we have in the city of Nagoya the firm of Nippon Toki whose 3300 workers turn out the famous Noritake line of plates, cups, saucers and other chinaware. Output is on the order of 1,750,000 pieces annually. Most of this output comes to the United States, where it sells for between $70 and $250 for a 93-piece dinner set.

Nippon Toki, in the spring of 1958, also entered into an agreement with the American firm Gladding, McBean of California to manufacture chinaware which Gladding will market in this country under its "Franciscan" brand.

Cameras are another line where the Japanese have recently emphasized quality, and the Nikon and Canon are usually rated as of equal quality with many of German and American manufacture. As early as 1957 Japan was exporting annually 3,200,000 cameras, about half to the United States. In that same year Japan's exports of sewing machines to the United States increased over the preceding year by 50 per cent, reaching $21 million in sales. Most of these machines were manufactured under contract to sell here with an American label.

Toys are another field being exploited by the Japanese. As with other products, the tendency here is also toward the higher-priced product. Much subcontracting is done, with toys bearing American labels being made in Japanese shops paying wage rates between 50 cents and 85 cents a day.

Other items of Japanese import include scooters, bicycles, binoculars, jewelry, tableware — the list is long. In June of 1959, *Oriental America,* a catalogue of Asiatic goods for export published by the East Asia Publishing Company in Tokyo, listed in its index over 250 advertisers. Some of these were in Hong Kong, but most were in Japan.

Today Japanese industry is merging, readying itself for the enormous drive for export markets which the nation must win in order to maintain economic life.

American officials had taken one look at Japan's postwar economy during the occupation period, and reached for the antitrust axe. Mitsui & Company, Ltd., is one example. In 1947 this was one of the world's greatest industrial combines. It held banks, mines, shipyards, chemical plants, heavy machinery factories, shipping and trading firms, and many other enterprises. At one time, just before World War II, Mitsui held 336 companies and had three million employees in Japan and overseas.

American authorities found nine major, family-controlled industrial empires which pretty much ran the economy of Japan. These were promptly dismantled. In all, forty-two holding companies were splintered, and dozens of industrial concerns were dissolved into small units. Thus did we plan to end the empire aristocracy of Japanese industry and turn it into our image of a democratic industrial state.

But the structure of a nation's industry reflects more than academic concepts of "competition" and "industrial democracy"; it is the outgrowth of a tradition and a social structure, and an expression of the will to grow and to survive. Our breaking up of the Japanese combines will in the long run probably be no more successful than in the case of Germany, where cartels once broken are reforming. Today the great Japanese firms are coalescing again — not quite in the same form as before, at least as yet, but the start is being made. Mitsui, for instance, is now only a trading company, but it holds contracts to buy the output of many of the firms it once controlled. This may well be the first step toward a re-establishment of ownership and control.

Thus we see emerging today a Japan which is challenging us in the markets of the world, and doing so with new strength, new products, new distribution techniques. Nor is the challenge only to us. Europe too is feeling the bite of competitive Japanese products. In the lobbies of Berlin's Kempinski Hotel, of the Park in Düsseldorf, in hotels in Paris, Rome and Milan, the small businessmen of the Orient move quickly and energetically about the business of building up the export trade of Nippon. By 1958 the Japanese were well into this European market, which was taking 10 per cent of their exports; and among the world exporters, Japan had moved up to fifth place.

In that year, Japan was also exporting capital and developing new sources for the raw materials for her industry to replace those lost in Manchuria in 1945.

To create the industrial base for such enterprise as the automobile makers Toyota and Nissan — both of which look toward the United States and world markets with their Toyoto and Datsun — Japan must import large quantities of iron ore, coal, pulp for fibers, and dozens of other raw materials. Within her own islands, resources of such materials are slim.

There are some observers who think that Japan will find her most economic raw material source in Alaska. Our forty-ninth state is 4000 miles from the Japanese industrial complex centering in Tokyo and Osaka. It is rich in many of Japan's raw material needs — wood pulp for paper and synthetic fibers, oil and probably many minerals, including coal and iron.

Actually the Japanese are already in Alaska with a $55.5-million pulp mill at Sitka, which was financed in part by a bond issue floated by the New York firm of Dillon Read. Alaska Pulp Company, Ltd., is owned by a group of Japanese corporations engaged in shipping and paper and rayon manufacture. It has under way at present also a large housing development. Executive offices are in Seattle, where there are two Japanese vice-presidents. But almost all employees are Americans. In this the owners of Alaska Pulp are following the custom of American firms with factories in Europe which as far as possible employ only the nationals of the countries where they have plants.

Japanese output of steel doubled between 1951 and 1957, reaching thirteen million tons in the latter year; and output will be on the order of eighteen million tons within the next three years. For this industry Japan needs coking coal, of which she has very little in her home islands. For some years one of the main sources of this vital raw material (which used to be brought from Manchuria) has been the Jewell Ridge Coal Corporation of Tazewell, Va., which has been shipping to Japan from its eastern United States field. Jewell is now studying the economics of developing mines in Alaska which would ship to Japan some three million tons of coking coal a year. Samples of the Alaskan coal have already been shipped to Japan for testing from the Bering River area along the glacial line near the Gulf of Alaska. Jewell holds prospecting permits covering over 10,000 acres of the most promising part of the field. Reserves are huge, enough to supply Japan's steelmaking and perhaps other coal needs for years. U. S. Government estimates put them at 1.1 billion tons of bituminous, and 2.1 billion of anthracite.

Other Japanese probes at the natural wealth of Alaska include exploration drillings for iron ore in the panhandle south of Juneau where ore was first discovered in 1956. This is being done by a company jointly financed by Japanese and American interests. A third group is looking into oil prospects, which in Alaska seem extraordinarily bright.

Oil is one of Japan's problems. She is the sixth largest user of petroleum products in the world, but has very limited supplies herself. In January of 1960 she announced a contract with the Soviet Union to take 1.5 million tons of crude over the next few years from the Baku fields.

It is an interesting speculation that Alaska may be more of an economic asset to Japan than to the United States. Most of the raw materials in that state are also available here, and at prices lower than they can be produced and shipped south from Alaska. But Japan, lacking such commodities herself and paying a much lower manufacturing wage than either Europe or the United States, could perhaps absorb a higher raw material cost than either of the other areas. Furthermore, Japan is much closer to Alaska, economically speaking, than appears from looking at a map. It is probably no more expensive to ship the 4000 miles across the Pacific than to most areas in the United States, where goods would have to be transhipped by rail from docks at Seattle.

The main areas for Japanese foreign investment, however, are Latin America and Asia, particularly Malaya and Thailand. Here Japanese investment is as heavy as it was back before World War II in Manchuria, Formosa and India. So prosperous is the domestic economy, so aggressive are the entrepreneurs of Tokyo and Osaka, and so large is current capital formation, that Japan in 1959 for the first time in her history became a creditor nation — was owed more money from abroad than she owed abroad — a position reached by the United States only as recently as 1916.

This then is the Japan with whose new economic strength we shall have to cope and with whom we shall have to find an economic live-and-let-live formula in the rising tide of production, investment and trade. In Europe we face the same necessity, although there the situation is somewhat different and probably dictates a different approach.

But in both areas the essential, basic problem is the same: how to deal with the economic forces which today tend to force the "meshing," the coming together into a new unity, of the various national economies of the industrial West. These forces are like a mighty current. They point, they sweep us, toward a free world economy . . . a world economy in which trade, investment and the movement of capital shall face no artificial barriers . . . in which various sorts of goods will be produced wherever they can be produced most cheaply and most efficiently . . . where markets are open to everyone on the same basis . . . where even labor, perhaps, shall move freely . . . where investment opportunities are everywhere open to all alike . . . and where national currencies are stable and freely exchangeable.

Such a world economy is of course the millennium. It will certainly not come in our lifetime, if it ever comes; but the forces that push us toward it are very real. The problem then is how to deal with those forces. It is discovering how far we can, or must, ride with them, and to what degree we have to thwart, delay or check them, in order to avoid economic explosion in the various nations concerned which might blow apart the whole political structure of the West.

The checks to these forces are tariffs, quotas both arbitrary and of the "voluntary" kind we have in Japan, and restrictions on investment, the movement of capital and the availability of foreign exchange. If these checks were to be abolished overnight, we would have economic chaos — for instance, in the case of electronics, we might see most of the industry move off lock, stock and barrel to Japan. On the other hand, there are many goods in which Japan is a high-cost producer — aluminum, some chemicals, medical instruments, to name just a few; and if all artificial barriers were abolished completely over a short period of time, the production of such goods would suddenly cease in Japan.

We shall return to this problem later in this book, after we have examined its aspect in Europe, particularly as exemplified in the two economic blocs which are now coming into being. Here it is only necessary to note that nationalism is dying as a way of economic life, and that we face the need of adjusting to the economic internationalism which presses for acceptance as the way of the future. This is a major adjustment that can hardly be made without some pain at some time to every nation concerned. It is therefore one which will test the political mettle of the modern democratic state, the ability of democratic man to look beyond his own narrow and immediate self-interest in order to build a new economic environment, a new prosperity, a new world peace.

XVI

"Creeping" Protectionism

THE TRADE POLICY of nations is an enormously complicated subject, but its importance cannot be overemphasized. Much of the world lives by foreign trade, and even in such relatively self-sufficient nations as the United States the in-and-out flow of goods can be a governing factor between prosperity and recession. As a generalization, trade policy can be either "liberal" — that is, favoring the fewest possible barriers and holding complete free trade as an ideal — or it can be "protectionist," which is the holding down of imports by tariffs and quotas to protect domestic industry against competition from overseas.

Most nations tend to be protectionists when they first become industrialized and infant industries need protecting. Mature manufacturing economies should, ideally at least, liberalize their trade barriers, buying goods from abroad in large amount so that they in turn can sell goods abroad in equal amount. This was the course that Britain followed from about the middle of the nineteenth century. It was the base of the British economy during that nation's most prosperous era, when British goods commanded the cream of the world market and the pound sterling in London was the ultimate currency of the business world. Britain still favors free trade. If in some instances and at various times she has had to compromise, usually this was the result of conditions brought about by protectionism in other nations which cut down their consumption of British goods; for the central fact of foreign trade is that a nation cannot expect to sell abroad unless in its turn it is prepared to buy from abroad. If a nation cannot earn dollars by selling goods in the United States, for instance, it does not have the dollars with which to buy goods in the United States. Thus the volume of imports to a large extent determines the volume of exports.

The United States was on the whole protectionist up to World War I, which was a logical policy for a nation building its industries and in a creditor position on balance. But during World War I, this changed. No longer did industry need coddling. Furthermore, we were owed more money than we owed, and people had to sell us the output of their mines, mills and factories in order to earn the dollars with which to service their debts to us. We, however, remained protectionist — first with the Fordney-McCumber Act of 1922, and later with the famous Hawley-Smoot Act of 1930.

The Hawley-Smoot law, which was vetoed by President Hoover but was passed over the veto by a protectionist-minded Congress, was a piece of unmitigated folly. It came at a time when the world economy was in a down-spiral anyway, and its provisions intensified the spiral into a vortex that sucked the economies of the free world down into the bleak years of the Great Depression. Obviously no single factor was responsible for the economic story of the 1930's, which bred so much individual suffering and political catastrophe. But most economists believe that our tariff policy contributed heavily to the disaster; for it erected barriers that dried up trade in every industrial nation in the world. At the same time it prevented Europe's earning the dollars here with which to service its heavy outstanding debts to us.

There are some, moreover, who will argue that if it had not been for the smothering economic effect of the Hawley-Smoot law, the recession that began with the crash of the New York Stock Market in 1929 might have run out its cyclical course in three instead of eleven years.

In 1934, however, largely owing to the economic vision and imagination of the hard-bitten old Tennessean, Cordell Hull, Secretary of State in the then new Roosevelt Administration, we saw and acted upon the errors of our ways. In that year Congress passed the Reciprocal Trade Agreements Act, under which, in subsequent years, we negotiated many tariff reductions with other nations. In fact, up until 1947, the United States moved steadily in the direction of freer trade.

But in the following year the first faint whiff of a returning protectionism was in the wind. Congress in 1948 renewed the Trade Agreements Act for only one year, instead of three, and introduced the so-called peril-point provision. This addition to the Act required that the Tariff Commission should report to the President on all items on which it was contemplating any tariff negotiation ". . . as to the limit to which such modifications might be extended without causing or threatening serious injury to domestic industries producing like or directly competitive articles."

The language of this provision was frighteningly broad to those supporting freer trade, and the new provision was dropped in 1949. Yet when Congress renewed the Act in 1951, it not only restored the peril-point clause, but added a tight "escape" clause. Also, protectionists succeeded in adding a gratuitous notice to the rest of the world that in renewing the Act Congress was not going on record as approving or disapproving GATT, the General Agreement on Tariffs and Trade, the organization under which tariff reductions are negotiated.

When the Act was again renewed in 1954, a provision was

written into it exempting the defense industries from tariff reductions. And in 1955, Congress still further tightened the peril-point and escape-clause provisions.

This tightening of our trade policy was very discouraging to our allies abroad. In 1950, when European and Japanese recovery seemed certain, hopes had been high of seeing an increasing volume of trade with the United States. Slowly these hopes were dashed by what freer-trade advocates called our "creeping protectionism."

European and Japanese businessmen had other reasons for discouragement. While we had come a long way in freeing trade in the preceding years — our average, over-all tariff rate, for instance, even now is only 11 per cent — we were still a difficult nation with which to do business. Foreign nations trying to trade with us have noted that much of our tariff reduction in recent years has been on goods in which we did not have to fear competition and was therefore of little practical advantage to them. A second complaint is that in the American import market another country "never knows where it stands," that a European firm may spend time and money developing a market in the United States and then, when the market had been opened, find a tariff suddenly thrown up in its face.

We have not, of course, been the only offenders. European nations, and particularly the Japanese, have barriers against dollar imports from this country. But in part these barriers were erected in the past when the nations concerned were attempting to rebuild their war-torn economies, and the purpose, at least in Europe, was often more to protect balance-of-payments position than to restrict the entry of goods. On the whole, Europe has moved steadily toward freeing trade whenever possible in recent years, particularly the Germans and British. Now we see the first steps in that direction even on the part of strongly nationalistic Japan.

Moreover, the initiative toward freer trade in the past

had to come from us, as the leading economic power. Not until the Treaty of Rome in 1957 and its subsequent implementation was there any other nation or group of nations of sufficient economic strength to exert any leadership in the reciprocal liberalizing of world trade.

But what is even more alarming to foreign nations today is that the protectionism that may be "creeping" as far as legislation goes is rising rapidly in the attitude of many American industries. Not in years has there been as much pressure on Congress and the administration for protection as there is today.

It is true, as noted in earlier chapters, that much American industry is building plant abroad, or importing parts from abroad, or licensing abroad, in order to meet foreign competition both in the world market and in the domestic market in the United States. But this is not true of all industries, nor of all companies within a certain industry. Furthermore, some companies are "playing the game from both ends," moving to produce goods abroad and urging protection of the domestic market at the same time.

In a sense there are two major forces playing on American industry at present: (1) the pressure to export production facilities to take advantage of lower-cost manufacture abroad, and (2) the pressure to protect our high-cost, high-price market in this country from the foreign invader. This dichotomy (which will be discussed more fully in a later chapter) gives much of industry's articulation of its purposes today a rather schizophrenic overtone, but it is very real and upon its resolution the future prosperity and stability of the free world may rest.

This brings us back to Europe, where in the formation of a second economic bloc in addition to the European Common Market there is emerging a situation of extraordinary intricacy with an outcome at present hard to foresee. At the moment, as in 1948, Europe is thinking in terms of a world of lower tariffs, fewer quotas, freer trade. But this could change, if we meet Europe's aspirations with no greater imagination than we have in the past.

In 1948 we had a great opportunity. We were then the economic giant . . . the sole giant; and we had it within our power to exert our leadership toward a freer world economy in which trade would be liberalized to the purpose of creating a truly new era for economic man. We chose to temporize, to compromise, and since then we have turned our face backwards a little toward the past. Today we have in a sense a second chance, but with this difference: that whereas we might have written the blueprints for the new era to suit ourselves in 1948, we must now draft them in consultation with others. We can still be chairman of the committee, if you like, but we must today be a chairman prepared to negotiate and to persuade.

XVII

Europe at "Sixes and Sevens"

THE TRADING SYSTEM of the British Commonwealth rests on two realities: that some, although not all, of the members of the Commonwealth grant each other preferential tariff rates; and that with only very few exceptions the goods of all Commonwealth nations can enter the United Kingdom duty-free.

It was this that prevented Britain from joining the European Common Market. The ECM was created with the purpose of abolishing over a period of years all tariffs between its six members, while at the same time the six would among themselves maintain a common tariff against other non-member nations.

If Britain were to join such a closed customs union, she would have to place a duty on a great many goods from Commonwealth nations which she now imports duty-free. This would have hurt the British economy, which demands the import of raw materials at as low a price as possible. It would have created a precedent for placing duties where none had existed before. It would have meant for Britain the abandoning of her whole Commonwealth system, which the British felt was a political impossibility. Above all, in British eyes it would have broken up the pattern of world trade and weakened the political ties of the underdeveloped areas with the Western world.

For these reasons the British were not signers of the Treaty of Rome in 1957. On the other hand, the British moved soon afterwards to explore the possibility of some arrangement under which they, along with other nations with which they had strong economic ties, might find an area of association with the ECM.

At that time Britain began to negotiate an economic group of her own in Europe which would not be a closed customs union like the ECM, yet would be a liberalizing factor in European trade. This group originally consisted of Britain, Norway, Sweden, Denmark, Switzerland and Austria. Later Portugal, long tied closely by trade to Britain, was added. This became the European Free Trade Area, known as FTA, a so-called Outer Seven, as opposed to the Inner Six of the ECM. Actually the FTA was not formally put together until the signing of the Stockholm Treaty in November of 1959; but it was with the group in mind that negotiations went on with the ECM during 1958.

These negotiations ran into trouble from the beginning. The difficulties were many and complex. For one thing, the ECM looked in the long run far beyond a customs union, in fact toward a European unity with common financial, economic and social policies, and with political federation as its eventual ideal. Neither Britain with her wide Commonwealth commitments nor the Scandinavian nations were prepared to go to such lengths. On the other hand, within the ECM was a great deal of reluctance to enter into any arrangement with non-ECM nations which would differ from those set up by the Rome Treaty — as, for instance, multilateral arrangements only designed to free trade — lest such arrangements weaken the ECM by diluting the whole concept on which it was based.

Another problem was that of France, long protectionist

by tradition. Perhaps this is too wide a generalization, but there was undoubtedly some truth in the commonly held belief that the purposes of Britain and France differed too much for reconciliation: that the British wanted to push free trade as far as it would go, whereas the French were thinking largely in terms of a new and enlarged protectionism which would include the whole Inner Six.

But behind these more obvious conflicts of interest there were many stumbling blocks. For instance, the size of the two groups may have caused Britain and the Scandinavian nations to hold back a little. The FTA population of ninety million was only half that of the ECM countries. (Production in the FTA is two-thirds of that of ECM, however.) Furthermore, the FTA area depended much more on overseas trade than did the ECM. It is true that roughly one-fourth of the trade of the Outer Seven is with the Inner Six. But it is also true that between 16 and 18 per cent of the trade of the Outer Seven is with each other, while 60 per cent of their trade is entirely outside Europe. At any rate, the negotiations broke down, and the FTA was put into treaty form finally in November of 1959.

Almost at once, a feeling of alarm swept the financial ministries of Europe and industrial and financial centers in the United States. The question which now loomed was this: was Europe, which had been moving so fast toward economic unity, now to turn to a new kind of sectionalism? Was the economic nationalism of the past now to be replaced, not by a unified Europe, but by a new kind of bloc system — a Europe split into two rival economic groups which might find themselves in a trade war not only with each other but with the United States?

American exporters wondered if they would find new barriers against American goods erected by both blocs. The Stockholm Treaty called for an across-the-board tariff cut of 20 per cent between FTA nations in mid-1960, and cuts of

10 per cent in each subsequent year. Yet each member was free to maintain against the outside world whatever barriers it wished.

This meant, of course, that goods coming in from outside would have to face a higher tariff than goods moving within the bloc: for instance, Scandinavian pulp and paper would have a lower duty to pay on entering Britain than would the same goods from the United States; or British machinery could enter Austria or Portugal at tariff rates lower than those for machinery from the United States. But this was not all. As noted in earlier chapters, American industry has invested heavily in new plant in Europe within the last few years. The purpose of this had been to secure a manufacturing base for the European and world markets which would be lower-cost than the United States, while at the same time having production facilities within the tariff walls of the ECM.

But a Europe in two blocs meant that goods produced within the ECM might have to face higher tariffs than previously in the FTA market, while goods produced in American-owned plant in Britain, for instance, might have the same problem in trying to penetrate the market of the Inner Six. This raised the possibility that American firms which had established plant in either the ECM, or in Britain or one of the other FTA nations, might soon have to duplicate those facilities in the other area in order to sell in both markets. And beyond that was the further rather ironic possibility that afterwards the two blocs might in the end come together in some form of trade agreement which would make such a duplication unnecessary and a waste of money — in fact, leave a company with too much European plant.

Plainly the European unity which the United States had urged so strongly for so long had taken a turn which could spell trouble. At stake was a huge overseas market for American goods. ECM nations took $2.4 billion in American ex-

ports in 1958, the FTA members $1.4 billion; while some
$5 billion of American direct investment in all Europe by
late 1959 was also now a matter for concern.

This situation was regarded as so serious that it was
brought up in the summit meetings in Paris in December,
when the way was paved for a meeting of economic ministries in the same city the following month. The British
were as much concerned as we. Selwyn Lloyd, Secretary of
State for Foreign Affairs, had been carrying on the negotiations with the ECM ministers, and he noted the "un-
pleasant undercurrent" in Europe that followed their breakdown in late 1958, a deterioration not only as between London and Paris, but London and Bonn, a "feeling of division,
almost of distrust."

Early in 1960, Lloyd spoke to the General Assembly of
the Council in Europe in Strasbourg and forcibly denied that
Britain was in any way opposed to the community of the
Inner Six. Britain was concerned over what she saw as the
political dangers that could lie in the ECM, however — the
formulating of policy on disarmament, for instance, or
Africa, or East-West relations, without prior consultation
with allies in NATO. If that happened, Mr. Lloyd said, he
did not see how Western European union could survive.

The French and also the Germans were said to have assured Lloyd that they were fully aware of such dangers and
that they had no intention of carrying on purely political
consultation of the sort he described. But the French at
least seem to have failed to convince the British minister that
they were thinking of freer trade in any broader perspective
than that prescribed by the Treaty of Rome for the Inner
Six, for Mr. Lloyd warned further at Strasbourg that if the
ECM should maintain high tariffs and remain protectionist
as against nonmembers, there would follow "trade war in
Western Europe," and that political cohesion would not
then survive.

The British were very anxious to state their case at this moment, perhaps because of the meetings in Paris where C. Douglas Dillon, Undersecretary of State for Economic Affairs, was trying to find means of preventing the swing of Europe to the two-bloc system.

Just two days before Lloyd's speech at Strasbourg, Reginald Maulding, President of the British Board of Trade, spoke before the Economic Club in New York. Maulding said that the political dangers of a divided Europe in times like these were "overwhelming," and he added:

"The Six and the Seven in their separate groups are going to abolish tariffs among themselves. We say the objective must be to abolish tariffs throughout Europe."

The British, with the support of many powerful groups in Germany, were setting the record clear. For over a century they had been free traders, at least to the degree that the policy of other nations, particularly the United States, had allowed them to be, and they believed that the trade problems of Western Europe could lead to political and economic friction which would weaken the whole free world.

Furthermore, they were looking beyond Europe. In the same talk before the Economic Club in New York, Maulding went on to voice a hope that the United States and Canada might join in such a system of freer trade. He knew the difficulties, he said, and the matter was of course one for Canada and the United States to decide. "But in the meantime," he continued, "I am sure you would not claim that we in Europe should halt our own progress. If we go ahead then by strengthening our own economies we shall once again be hastening the time when we can further expand our trade with you. In other words, I do not think it is good for us or for you that the pace of the removal of tariff barriers in Europe should be tied to the pace at which you can agree to remove trade barriers between you and us."

We would like you to join with us in freeing world trade

and working toward a new economic unity, Maulding was saying in effect; but if you do not do this, then do not ask us to hold back, for we shall go on without you.

Dillon had already arrived in Paris when these words were spoken, where he had proposed a wider trade group consisting of all members of the OEEC, plus the United States and Canada. The exact functioning of this organization was not defined at the time, except that it would supplant the OEEC, which many felt had outlived its usefulness and should now be replaced with another organization more rigidly directed toward the economic problems looming over the NATO powers.

Maulding's words were significant, for he was holding up the possibility of some form of Atlantic economic community in which the United States and Canada would hold membership and which would contain, of course, the Outer Seven and the Inner Six. Here was a vision to catch the imagination. A community of nations which would contain over three-quarters of the world's industrial strength. This would be a true coalescing of the economic power of the West.

How realistic is this vision?

This is a question which in the next few years will be answered by the workers, industrialists and politicians of the United States.

XVIII

Four Wise Men

Iᴛ ᴡᴀѕ perhaps unfortunate that in 1959 and early in 1960 the two most powerful statesmen in continental Europe were men for whom economics in its modern sense is pretty much of a closed book — de Gaulle and Adenauer. This has also been true of recent American Presidents, but Roosevelt, Truman and Eisenhower had about them men whose understanding of the world today was framed in reality, even if it was not invariably profound, and all three Presidents were willing to take economic advice.

Adenauer and de Gaulle, however, are both caught up in a myth which has bound them to each other in a strong affinity — the myth that through strength and determination the West can force the Soviet Union to relinquish its East German satellite, that Germany can remain a partner in NATO and at the same time reunify its West and East segments.

Adenauer has staked his political future on his ability to make the German people continue to believe in this myth. De Gaulle, of course, does not believe in it, but he is said to have supported Adenauer in return for the German Chancellor's backing in his uncompromising economic policy toward the Outer Seven. Actually de Gaulle could have no desire to see a unified Germany. He almost certainly would prefer a rearmed West Germany allied to France, rather than a neutralized united Germany which might prove unpredictable in the coming decade.

The political alliance which thus imprisons these two strong figures is unfortunate, despite the fact that without de Gaulle's strength and quality as a leader France might never have instituted the monetary and fiscal policies which made possible the cohesion of the Inner Six. It has strengthened the French hand which holds back from liberalization of trade outside the ECM nations. Furthermore, it was back of Adenauer's recent effort to destroy politically his liberal-minded and imaginative Finance Minister Erhard who, with the backing of most of Germany's heavy and important industry, has long looked for economic union far more inclusive than that of the ECM. De Gaulle and Adenauer are the axis of power in Europe today, yet both men fail to realize that perhaps the major truth of modern times is that the economic and political objectives of nations are indivisible. *Grandeur pour la patrie* is all very well, but it cannot in these days be paid for by a lack of bread.

The meetings in Paris in January 1960 were probably historic. Writing of them at the time, Edgar L. Dale, Jr., of the *New York Times* asked these questions: What does the United States want? Has there been a change in the world economic situation? Is there something wrong that needs curing?

The last two questions were rhetorical. The economic situation was changing almost from month to month and had been for three years; and the "something that needed curing" were the frictions which threatened to split Europe into a two-bloc economy.

What did the United States want? The answer seems easy enough: for the free world we wanted economic growth in an inflation-free economy; and for ourselves we wanted to sell more goods abroad to further prosperity at home and to help correct the deficit in our balance-of-foreign-payments position. But while the broad goals were easy to define, the means to their attainment were illusive in a Europe under the shadow of de Gaulle and Adenauer.

Dillon's suggestion was to reorganize the Organization for European Economic Cooperation or to create a new organization to supplant it. The OEEC had been set up originally after World War II to channel American economic aid. Its membership consisted of the eighteen major countries of Europe, with the United States and Canada sitting in only as observers. The new group would include the two North American powers as full members, and its broad purposes would be to encourage transatlantic trade and to increase European aid to the underdeveloped areas.

Four "wise men" were appointed and instructed to report on April 18 on the structure of the new organization. There were W. Randolph Burgess, once Assistant Secretary of the Treasury and currently serving as U. S. Ambassador to NATO; Sir Paul Gore-Booth of Britain, formerly attached to the Embassy in Washington; Bernard Clappier of France; and Xenophon Zolotas of Greece.

Later, on March 1, Burgess gave a little clearer picture of what the "wise men" were thinking. This was of an organization which would: consult regularly on policies, and seek to promote economic growth and financial stability; consider trade policies, although without infringing on GATT (General Agreement on Tariffs and Trade), and without creating new trading arrangements; foster consultations and coordination among nations in a position to aid in the development of the underdeveloped areas; continue the work of the OEEC in the field of science and energy.

Mention was made of the contest between the Soviet Union and the free world being more than ever economic, and the problem of the underdeveloped areas was given full attention. Burgess did not state the position of this country on whether the new group should have the power of decision, or be merely consultive; but the *New York Times* stated that "those associated with economic policies in the State Department are believed to favor such powers [of decision] strongly, provided they do not commit the United States in advance to policies requiring Congressional approval and that decisions require unanimous agreement."

The thought that occurs, of course, is that without real policy-making powers, the new organization could be little more than a club where members will discuss the economic policies of nations and offer plans, protests and suggestions. Yet it may be too early to tell. The pressure of European events on the United States has been running strong in recent months, and is likely to intensify. Europe is speaking softly, but in its new economic strength and industrial power it carries a very persuasive stick.

De Gaulle and Adenauer are old men, and the status of the former is always subject to France's historical political instability. Behind these two men, who unquestionably are thinking in terms of a "little" Europe — a Europe led economically by Germany and France, and protectionist as beyond the confines of the ECM — are men with wider economic vision. Minister of Economics Ludwig Erhard in Germany, denied the chancellorship by Adenauer, has the backing of the most powerful industrial voices in Germany in his ideal of a great, broad Atlantic Economic Community which would eventually absorb the Outer Seven and the Inner Six and in effect bind the free world together in a new economic unity of the whole West.

In France, the picture is less clear, and in the banks of Europe the question, "After de Gaulle, what?" is on everyone's lips. Yet it is perhaps significant that Antoine Pinay was dropped by de Gaulle in late 1959 when the summit and economic meetings were occupying the center of the Eu-

ropean stage. Pinay, as Finance Minister, was the real architect of France's economic stability. He is strongly backed by
the Patronat Français and, probably, by most of French
heavy industry. Pinay has never expressed himself on the
issue of the limited ECM versus a wider economic community. But it may well be that there is mounting in France a
body of influential opinion which takes the Erhard view
rather than that of Adenauer and de Gaulle.

One reason for this could be the enormous strengthening
of France's price position in the world market following the
stabilizing and devaluation of the franc.

The devaluation had the effect, of course, of raising domestic prices — a part of the belt-tightening de Gaulle asked
of the French people. But at the same time it lowered
France's export prices, as dollars, pounds and marks bought
more francs with which to make payment for goods for export. French steel, for instance, was underselling German
steel during the inflow to the United States for stockpiling
prior to the steel strike. French computers are more than
competitive. In fact, never before have German and British
companies been given a stiffer run for their money by the
French than in the past year and a half in European markets,
and the new strength of France's export position may well
slowly erode the protectionism traditional to that country —
a protectionism which to a certain extent imprisons the
thinking of de Gaulle today. It is axiomatic that the competitive position of industry measures the tolerance of the
freeing of a nation's trade. Belgium, Holland and Luxembourg have always favored a minimum of protection, and
would certainly have everything to gain and almost nothing
to lose by a wider and more inclusive economic unity.
Among the Inner Six, this leaves only Italy, whose economic
recovery and new strength is in many ways the most remarkable in Europe.

In the past, Italy has been ranged with France as generally

protectionist, and she still stands in that role to a certain extent. But this may be passing. Two years ago, Italy seemed to be at a disadvantage within the ECM as against the basically very rich economy of France and the much-publicized economic power of West Germany. But the Italians soon showed they could more than deal with the French and Germans on equal terms.

Italy's gross national product reached its prewar level in 1949, and has been increasing ever since at an average rate of 5 per cent a year — even in the recession of 1958, it rose by 4.1 per cent. This same year saw the turning point fiscally or financially.

In 1957 Italy showed a deficit on her trade account of $880 million (the excess of imports over exports). But in 1958 that deficit had been shrunk to only $437 million. This meant that Italy was riding very high in the matter of her over-all balance-of-payments position, for the smaller deficit was a great deal more than offset by an income of $230 million from shipping, by tourist spending in Italy of $414 million and by $260 million in remittances sent home by emigrants.

The over-all balance-of-payments surplus in 1957 was a slender $4 million . . . but it was a very comfortable $565 million in the following year. As a result, Italy's gold and dollar reserves rose in that one year by $900 million to a total of over $2.2 billion. These reserves ranked fourth among the trading nations of the world, relatively, exceeded only by those of Canada, West Germany and the United States. With such backing, plus high industrial activity, the lira has become one of the soundest currencies in Europe, with a tendency at times to sell at a premium as against the pound and even the dollar.

Furthermore, Italy has today an enormous economic asset in what was once her great problem — her underdeveloped south. Throughout Europe today labor is the problem, the bottleneck to further economic growth. Unemployment is less than ¼ of 1 per cent of the labor force in West Germany, for instance. It is almost as tight in Holland, and only a little less so in France. But in Naples and to the south, Italy has a pool of some 1.7 million unemployed workers upon which she can draw as her industrial development continues.

Finally there is the recent strengthening of the position of Italian exports in the European market. Italian labor is extremely good — particularly in the newer industries like electronics where women are skilled at the light assembly work. In 1957, West Germany was the competitor everyone in Europe feared, and the industries of the Ruhr and Rhine valleys were extremely confident of their competitive position. This is true no longer. It is the Italians who are pushing north, into France, into Germany, into the Low Countries with their textiles, their electrical and electronic products, their appliances.

Actually, Italy, with low manufacturing costs and with the surplus labor which will allow large industrial expansion, will almost inevitably show a much greater relative growth than either France or Germany in the next decade. And with this and their strong cost position, the Italians almost certainly will tend to move steadily toward a broader and freer trade policy — toward the British position, in other words.

Thus it is hard to see over a period of time any outcome in Europe other than a gradual discovery of common purpose and common opportunities between the members of the Outer Seven and the Inner Six. It may not come quickly, and certainly there will be problems, divisions, difficulties to be faced. But the same basic forces which exert pressure for unity and the meshing of the economies of the whole free world in a broader sense, are at work in Europe in a much more limited and closely contained area. These forces may

be resisted, thwarted for a time. But sooner or later they
will prove irresistible, and the Inner Six and the Outer
Seven will become the Thirteen — or perhaps the Eighteen
as the fringe nations of Europe are drawn in.

While it was the danger of a splitting of Europe into two
blocs which led Dillon, speaking for the United States, to
propose in Paris in January of 1960 the formation of a new
group to supplant the OEEC, it may well be that the future
will spell out a different danger for this country — a Europe
strongly united into one bloc and independent of the United
States.

Much had been made of the disadvantage this country
would face by finding itself shut off by tariff walls from a
two-bloc Europe; but surely the disadvantage would be even
greater if we were to find ourselves shut off from a Europe
organized into one bloc and for that reason all the more
economically powerful. This is particularly true because
of the rising industrial strength and the new economic internationalism of the Soviet Union. To the extent that we
are removed from European trade, the Soviet Union may
well in future years move in, both as a supplier of raw materials and as a huge new market for manufactured products.

XIX

A New Soviet Voice?

THE GROWTH of the Soviet Union's economy has been directed and stimulated by a series of Five-Year Plans, of which, all told, there were six. The last of these, formulated in 1954 and designed to chart the economy from 1955 through 1961, was dropped in 1957, however. To replace it, the 21st Party Congress which met in February of 1959 adopted a new Seven-Year Plan, which was drawn up to fit into broader fifteen-year goals.

This new plan made several administrative changes. It set up annual goals to replace the old five-year goals. It tightened administration in various ways, and at the same time placed greater responsibility on local and regional officials. The architect of these changes is generally believed to have been Nikita Khrushchev himself; and the extent of the reorganization is indicated by the fact that in 1957 and 1958 over twenty ministries of industry were abolished in Moscow.

The Soviet Master Plan — fifteen years, as distinct from the Seven-Year Plan now in operation — is a remarkable document. As announced by the Soviet Embassy in London in March, 1960, it set out the following broad goals:

The "complete" electrification of Russia.

"Comprehensive" automation of production.

Seven-fold expansion of electric power (which would give the Soviet Union approximately 1.5 billion kilowatts of capacity, roughly twice that of the United States at present).

Coal production of 750 million tons (greater than that of all Europe in 1958).

An output of 300 million tons of iron ore.

Perhaps such plans are too grandiose to be realistic; but remember that the Soviet Union is unique among nations in that it can control absolutely the allocation of production as between consumer goods and capital goods — in other words, it can hold down the living standards of its people in order to provide a high rate of investment in the capital area.

The intermediate Seven-Year Plan itself envisages an over-all capital investment of two trillion rubles or roughly $500 billion, a capital investment greater than that of the United States in the past twenty years.

Steel production is slated to rise from 36 million tons to 90 million . . . oil production from 113 million metric tons to 240 million . . . electric power from 233 billion kilowatt hours to 520 billion . . . and so it goes. Over-all industrial output is to increase by between 85 and 88 per cent.

Consumer goods are also expected to show a dramatic increase. Milk, meat and egg production is to exceed that of the United States by 1965. Shoe output is to rise from 356 million pairs to 515 million; that of silk-type fabrics, from 845 million yards to 1.5 billion.

Most European economists see nothing very unrealistic in these goals and believe that their attainment would mean the emergence of the U.S.S.R. as the world's strongest economic power. Europe and the United States at the end of the Seven-Year Plan will each have total output greater than that of the Soviet Union, quantitively. But whereas much of European and American production of steel, copper, electric power and oil finds its way into actually non-essential consumer goods, the Soviet Union will be throwing her production of these industries largely into railroads, machinery for factories, bridges, building.

Figures on automobile production in the U.S.S.R., for instance, are not even published, and the nation produced only 360,000 refrigerators in 1958. Russian output is concentrated in industrial plant and armaments, the sinews and muscle of economic and political strength.

Such a growth would have a powerful capillary attraction for a newly united European economy. From Europe the Soviet Union could buy consumer goods, machinery for her factories, turbines, chemical plants, the pipe for her oil lines which are already building from the fields at Baku toward terminals on the borders of the Iron Curtain. To Europe, the Soviet Union could sell metals, hides, food and feed grains, lumber, pulp and many other raw materials.

Such trade opportunities might be hard if not impossible for Europe to resist; for to a degree sometimes hard for us in this country to grasp, the economy of Europe lives by trade. In a gross national product for all Western Europe of $300 billion, exports in 1959 amounted to $43 billion; whereas in the United States with a gross national product of $484 billion, only $17.6 billion in goods were exported.

In the past, foreign trade has been even less important to the Soviet Union than to the United States — exports stood at only $4.4 billion in 1959. But this is changing. Either out of economic need, or because of the political advantages to be obtained, the officials of the Kremlin are making today a strong bid to place the U.S.S.R. among the world's trading nations. This is much publicized in the visits of such men as Deputy Premier Mikoyan to Mexico, Cuba, even the United States, but the real bid for markets and the offer of raw materials are being made quietly in Europe.

Soviet emissaries have bought much equipment in Britain — chemical plants, sugar beet factories, rubber plants. In return the Russians are exploring the British market for softwoods, and metals are sold in large amounts at times in the London markets. There is even talk of Soviet cameras and automobiles. On May 24, 1959, the British and the Soviets signed a trade agreement under which Russia expects to take almost $2 billion in British goods over the following two years. Actually in May and June of that year alone, a total of $112 million worth of capital goods was sold to the U.S.S.R. by British firms.

Forecast is hazardous where account must be taken of the policy of the Kremlin, but there is at least a strong possibility that in the next decade we shall see an intensification of such efforts, with Soviet trade emissaries moving through Europe with offers that industry in this country would not be able to meet.

In early March of 1960, *U. S. News & World Report* published an article which asked the question: "WHOSE CENTURY? Will it be Russia's? . . . Will it be Europe's? . . . Will it be America's?"

Beneath this title, the magazine ran in a box the following statement:

Suddenly, in the midst of a century that was to be America's, a new challenge appears.

The challenger? Not the Soviet Union. It is Western Europe.

Only a decade ago, U. S. was pouring billions in aid into a bankrupt Europe. Since then, Europe's free nations have made a big comeback. Today, they are outstripping Russia in production, gaining on U. S.

Is a "Third force" emerging? Has U. S. aid created a dangerous rival?

Add up the facts and you find: U. S. is still ahead. And the challenger, Western Europe, is on the American side.

This is all very well, and it is very comforting to think that Europe, "the challenger," is on our side. Europe is certainly on our side now, and likely to remain so, ideologically. But remember that the Europeans, by and large, believe that the Soviet Union will discover her main antagonist, not to the West, but in Red China . . .

That Europeans are very knowledgeable and do not believe that the second strongest national economy in the world can be contained by an economic *cordon sanitaire* . . .

That most of Europe thinks that rich nations do not start wars in the modern world and that the best chance for world peace lies in a situation in which Russia will attain her economic goals and emerge with an industrial complex capable of supplying higher living standards for her people.

It is for these reasons that the Europeans have never seen eye-to-eye with us on doing business with the Soviet Union. When Russia has tried to buy certain goods here and has been refused, she has supplied her needs without difficulty in Europe—in chemical manufacturing equipment, for instance, from Italy's Montecatini or the British firms of Courtauld's and Vickers Armstrong. The oil from the Baku fields, as another illustration, flows northward toward Central Europe through Italian pipe.

Thus it is easy to envisage Europe, "the challenger," still being firmly on our side ideologically and by sentiment and tradition, yet being drawn slowly away from us and closer to the Soviet Union through economic forces. The vision is an alarming one, replete with irony. But it represents a danger that is very real.

In the first place, there is the rate of economic growth. Today the output of goods in all of Western Europe is about 60 per cent of that of the United States, and Soviet output stands at a little less than 50 per cent.

But by 1970, according to estimates of the OEEC, Western Europe will be producing at 70 per cent of our output, and the Soviet Union at 60 per cent.

Europe and the Soviet Union are both growing more

rapidly than we, and a certain mutual economic attraction will be established by that very fact.

There is also the danger that Europe, always on the search for new markets for manufactured products and cheaper sources of raw material, may find in the Soviet Union a more satisfactory trading partner than in the United States. Costs in the Soviet Union are very low, and can even be ignored if in so doing the Kremlin can discover a political or even long-term economic advantage. The Russians, in other words, can sell Europe whatever it suits them to sell, and at any price they please. They are equally flexible in the purchase of European goods. Thus they have it in their power to establish with the industries of Western Europe a very close economic association, built on mutually desirable trade.

This prospect is truly frightening, for it holds within it the possibility of gradual meshing of the economies of Europe and the Soviet Union, instead of those of Europe and the United States. Such a development would leave this country economically isolated, at least to a great degree, and it could reduce us to the status of a second-rate economic power in the course of a few years. It is all the more frightening when measured against the rise of protectionist voices in this country at present. For if we do not buy from Europe, Europe will not buy from us. If we do not buy from Europe, the Soviet Union will undoubtedly do so, and will sell Europe its raw materials in return.

It will be argued that the above is stretching more than a little, and that the danger is more fanciful than real. Perhaps. But there is one curious fact which in the last two years has aroused a great deal of interest in European central banks. This, as noted in an earlier chapter, is that the gold with which the Soviet Union settles its international accounts is superbly packaged, extremely satisfactory for a bank to handle, and often underassayed — *i.e.,* containing just a little more gold than official measurement. This has raised a question in Europe: Has the Soviet Union some dramatic monetary move in mind?

No one knows exactly the extent of Soviet gold holdings, but estimates range from $8 billion to $12 billion. Furthermore, the U.S.S.R. is the second largest producer of gold today, crowding close on South Africa.

Now suppose, with this gold reserve, the Kremlin were to make the ruble fully convertible — convertible not only into gold but into other currencies — in other words, were to launch the ruble among the other world currencies. Many believe that such is Russia's plan, and that she awaits simply the psychological moment for its launching. A prerequisite to such a move, of course, would be a greater degree of confidence in the financial integrity of Soviet policy than probably exists at the moment. On the other hand, any action on our part which might raise questions as to ability or intention to defend the dollar would play directly into Soviet hands.

It is interesting to speculate that under certain circumstances such a move might establish the ruble as the soundest, the hardest currency on earth.

Russia's gold stocks are all "free." No foreign balances stand as a call on them; no gold need be kept aside by law as a currency reserve. But it is not the gold backing alone which could make the ruble strong under such conditions. More than gold is behind a national currency; and a ruble fully convertible would be backed by the huge, low-cost resources of Russia — her factories, her forests, her farm lands, her oil fields, her mines.

Today we are much concerned with the possibility of losing the Cold War in the underdeveloped areas of the world. We see a threat in Soviet trade and aid arrangements in India and Latin America. We think of the contest as one in which we shall have to "win the minds and allegiance" of the people of these lands.

In this, we may be making a serious mistake. Indeed, if the Kremlin commands the economic brain power which we must assume it does, the current Soviet moves in the underdeveloped areas may be simply diversionary tactics, steps to keep the pot boiling until the situation in Europe ripens. For Europe — with its huge rate of growth, its vast resources of technical and scientific skills, its superb industrial plant — is the crucial area.

In the world today economic forces are rising in flood tide, and the ideological differences which have hitherto kept peoples apart are in ebb. Stalin is dead, and the fire has gone out of Marxist doctrine. The Russia of today may use the vocabulary of Marx, but in international economics it moves along paths which would not seem too strange to Adam Smith.

Is the Europe we helped "save from Communism" in the Marshall Plan of 1948 now to discover in the Soviet Union a closer and more mutually profitable economic relationship than it can find in the United States?

That is a question that in large part the people of the United States themselves will answer. We will answer it in our policies on trade and foreign investment, in the wisdom with which we adjust our traditional economic attitudes to the realities of the coming decade.

XX

Trade Wars Are for Keeps

W HILE THE STATESMEN of the Western powers were sitting down in Paris to the problems of the FTA and ECM, the 87th Congress convened in Washington with its attention focused on the coming elections in November and its ears echoing with prophecy that the nation was entering its greatest decade.

University and business economists almost unanimously saw ahead great prosperity, which was to be realized through the marvels of science acting upon a large population growth. Personal incomes were to rise. Production was to increase. Science was the new frontier in these "Fabulous" or "Soaring" or otherwise wonderful Sixties in which man was to face both his greatest opportunity and his greatest challenge in the reaches of space.

To be sure, on the very day that Congress convened, the Dow-Jones industrial averages reached their all-time high — as of this writing — and promptly started a decline which in ninety days carried them down some 14 per cent and shaved many billions of dollars in value off the shares listed on the New York Exchange. Detroit too failed in the early months of the year to reach its expected volume. Steel shortages left by the strike in 1959 proved to be a great deal less than had been estimated. And housing starts stumbled into a quite sharp decline.

Such hesitancies in the economy gave no very serious concern, however. Business might be a little sticky at the moment. But what of it? Unlike Europeans, who will settle for an estimate as to how business will look four to six months ahead, American industry loves greatly the long-term outlook and prognostication, and only the prophets of "gloom and doom" would question that in 1970 the nation would be much richer and stronger than ever.

This may well turn out to be very good prophecy, for the United States does have in its hands the chance to play a large part in forming a brave new economic world. But the almost unanimous note of optimistic prediction was nevertheless alarming, for it ignored the forces that came into play with the close of the Korean conflict. It assumed that the problems of the present were not too different from those of the past, and hence, that policies proved sound in the past would remain so in the future — with but minor variations.

The world economy which today emerges is as different from that of any previous era as an Atlas missile from a B-29.

In the 1930's, the industrial nations discovered that production of goods was no longer a problem. Unlike previous depressions, the crisis of those years was not caused by insufficient production, but by the ability to produce more goods than we could distribute under the system then in force. Thus the politically explosive paradox of that era when men walked the streets jobless and in want, while factories shut down because of surplus inventories of goods. The problem of those years was to find means under the then existing system of getting the output of farms and factories into consumers' hands.

We did not solve that problem. It was solved by World

War II, which reversed the situation and forced us to strain every industrial sinew to maximum production to provide weapons and support the military and civilian population during the war.

Then came the 1950's, when the problem was to rebuild, and the great question to be answered was whether the overproduction brought about by war was to result in the inevitable crash which had always hitherto followed major conflicts. We met and solved the problem of rebuilding, and in so doing we may very well have avoided a postwar depression. Who knows the extent to which the reequipping of factories in Japan and Europe may have bolstered the domestic economy? Every dollar sent abroad in aid or credit returns sooner or later to be spent in the United States. The Marshall Plan not only paid off in aiding the rebuilding of Europe, it added to prosperity here.

Then too we had learned new anticyclical techniques, means of countering a business downturn: the dropping of money rates and the unbalancing of the federal budget through heavy public spending to check an impending economic decline. Thus, all in all, the confidence with which we face the 1960's seemed justified by the record. We had not done badly with our economic policy during the past twenty years. We had solved the problems of production, and the problems of distribution, and perhaps even the problems of economic stability. The "ifs" were fading, and ours was the world and everything that was in it. The decks were cleared for the stab at the stars.

But questioning this happy state of mind is a profound truth of which we are as yet only somewhat fuzzily aware. This was phrased by Edgar L. Dale, Jr., of the *New York Times*, during the meeting in Paris as follows: ". . . the economic and political objectives of nations are becoming synonymous." Carried a little further, the proposition might be stated thus: that politics today is a reflection of economic conflicts and objectives, and that economics has hence radically altered the complexion of politics.

Yet newspaper editors in the United States still treat elections in large part as a sort of popularity contest between those carrying the banners of the Democratic Donkey and the Republican Elephant. Political writers report polls, opinion surveys and the utterings of party chairmen as maneuvers in the "great game." And politicians rise to deliver themselves of propositions, opinions and proposals which, except as they may influence a few votes on election day, seem quite unrealistic and sometimes a little absurd.

This is not true in Europe, where issues are usually clearly defined, and it is unfortunate that it should be so in the United States, for today we with the rest of the world are swept along in a current of events which will have little tolerance for the parochialism of politicians or a naïve press.

The economic issue of the 1960's will be not production, nor distribution, nor even stability, as it has been successively in the past three decades. It will be organization — the problem of how the world economy is to be organized economically in terms of investment, money, trade. To the extent that politics reflects this fact, it will operate realistically. The danger lies in our assuming that the problems of today are the same as those of yesterday, and that solutions may be sought in variations of policies that may have worked in the past.

As of this writing, for instance, there is a strong likelihood that monetary policy may very soon become a political issue, that the call may go out for "cheaper" money. To a certain extent this depends on the course of the economy. If we maintain a high degree of prosperity, the call will be muted, for it will seem that the present Federal Reserve policy has been wise. If on the other hand we run into even a mild recession, the demand will rise strongly for all the countercyclical weapons, including particularly lower interest rates and public spending on an order such as will produce a large budgetary deficit. For this, after all, was the medicine that worked so well in 1957-58, so why not try it again?

The reason why it cannot be tried again — without, that is, exposing the nation to a very real danger — has been in part outlined in previous chapters: in the modern world no nation running a deficit in foreign account, as we are at present, can afford to allow the impression that it will not or cannot defend the integrity of its currency. But the danger is compounded by the situation emerging in Europe vis-à-vis the Soviet Union. For if by any chance the Soviet Union is nursing its gold with the thought of making the ruble convertible, here certainly would be the moment, the golden chance.

Picture a situation in which low interest rates here would make it more profitable for Europeans to repatriate their short-term balances to Europe, plus a large deficit in the federal budget and a consequent inflationary surge that would make holders of dollars think that our currency would in the future be worth less than it is today. Suppose now that in this situation the Kremlin were to announce the free convertibility of the ruble, gold-backed, and offer to sell to Europe raw materials at a price level which we in this country could not meet.

The effect would be an economic explosion that could split apart the whole West. If the chance of such a maneuver seems farfetched, so also did the ability of the Allied powers to produce a nuclear explosion seem to the Kremlin in 1945. Winston Churchill has said that when Stalin was first told of the Chicago project, he did not seem to grasp what it meant.

If the Cold War is in truth essentially an economic conflict, we shall certainly be taking a grave chance with the national security if we assume that the Soviet Union will play by the rules set up when full employment and individual national prosperity were the principal objectives of every country's economic policy. Such are not the main objectives of the Kremlin, which today thinks of economics as an instrument to world power; and one of the harsher realities we shall soon face is that we may have to at least lower the priority of such objectives in our thinking. The struggle for economic power is confining to history the whole philosophy which saw the ultimate purpose of economic policy as a perpetually rising standard of living protected by the provisions of a welfare state.

Economic power today is being employed as military power is applied, ruthlessly and under the concept that the end justifies the means. While the process is just beginning, it is almost certain to accelerate as Europe, Japan and the Soviet Union put on industrial muscle at a more rapid rate than we. Furthermore, it is not only the Soviet Union which will play rough in the decade we are now entering. Trade is economic life to Japan and Europe, and few nations have hesitated to go to war for economic advantage in the past. While the military art has become so destructive that war is today too expensive even for the victor, this only means that the weapons have changed. Quotas have taken the place of battleships; and tariffs, of battalions.

This is something which it will be difficult for this country to grasp fully. We have become conditioned to think of economic competition between nations as a broadened version of the competition between two companies whose presidents sit down together at bridge in the evening and josh each other about an order lost, or an order won. In part this is because of our historic isolation and our relatively smaller dependence on trade. But it is also because, for the first time within the memory of most political and business leaders, we are no longer too strong to be challenged, because we are no longer the sole economic giant.

Here then is the danger today: unless we can join with other nations in setting up some kind of an organization of the free world economy which will allow a gradual meshing of the various national economies, we shall find ourselves slowly isolated — or driven into an economic conflict that could wreck our economy in the course of a few years.

The danger is very real. *Trade war* may sound to an American businessman like an overworked journalist's term, but to the European it has literal meaning. It is a struggle for economic life in which there are no ethics and few loyalties. Here we would be playing for keeps.

XXI

The World Companies

THE POSITION in which the United States found itself in late 1959 and early 1960 as regards monetary policy and our balance-of-payments deficit gave many a conservative economist a chance to laugh up his sleeve. For a generation bankers, businessmen and sound-money advocates had been warning of the dangers of inflation and other forms of economic pain which lay in our following the economic philosophy of the high-spending, budget-careless welfare state.

Yet, despite these warnings, the nation had prospered. In the depression of the 1930's, the "new" economics had apparently justified itself; it had at least prevented the depression of that era from plunging deeper than it had. With less justification, the same economic approach had been followed in the postwar years. But who knew, after all, if it was not this which had saved us from the severe downturn which had always followed war in the past? We had paid for this with inflation, of course — roughly a 20 per cent loss of value in the dollar. But was the price too high? Many said no, pointing to the rising wage level that protected most workers, or at least postponed the ill effects. In fact, some economists were either resigned to or actively espoused a slow, year-to-year inflation as the only way of maintaining full employment and avoiding economic stagnation or decline.

But now suddenly the conservatives were being proved right. The wolf they had been crying for so long had now put in an appearance. It was there, incorporated in our foreign payments deficit and the insistence on hard money by nations overseas.

If the politicians were slow in recognizing this, or preferred not to recognize it in an election year, the opposite was true of sound-money advocates, who saw now in their hands a club with which to beat their antagonists who had seemed to be proving them wrong for so many past years. Hardly a stockholders' report of an insurance company or a bank went out in early 1960 that did not call attention in one way or another to the danger, warning that without balanced budgets and "realistic" interest rates the dollar might be put in jeopardy. Regardless of the past, we had now come to the end of the road. We had no more excess economic muscle to be wasted, no more economic fat.

Industry too was having its own last laugh. For years labor spokesmen had been insisting that union action in forcing ever-higher wages was partly responsible for our huge prosperity. Their argument had been that high wages meant high purchasing power . . . that high purchasing power was indivisible from the mass-production, mass-market economy of the nation . . . and that only through ever-mounting wage levels could industry be forced to the large capital investment in plant that was itself perhaps the greatest of all instruments to generally prosperous times.

But now industrialists could point to the world market, and to our own market here. Imports of foreign goods had been up in 1959 by $2.5 billion, whereas our exports had risen by only $150 million. This was largely the result of cost differentials, which was another way of saying wage differentials. We were losing markets, which would sooner or later mean the loss of jobs, through the heights to which monopolistic labor unions had forced the hourly wage.

"As inflation has pushed our general price level higher and higher, more and more of our buyers will make trips abroad this year," said John A. Barr, chairman of the big mail-order house, Montgomery Ward, in an address at the Harvard Business School in March, 1960.

"We would much prefer to buy American goods," Barr continued. "But we are being forced to buy foreign merchandise because such goods better suit our customers' needs. Our competitors are buying more foreign goods and our customers are indicating a preference for such goods simply because they want the best value for themselves.

"The evil of this is that it means less production and consequently fewer jobs. It is high time and extremely urgent that organized labor recognized the seriousness of this menace."

Thus spoke one of the nation's largest buyers of merchandise, one of the best customers for the output of literally hundreds of factories, a company selling at retail some $1.2 billion worth of goods a year.

Two days before Barr spoke, a more veiled warning was delivered at the Chicago World Trade Conference. This was the statement by Francis X. White, vice-president of American Machine & Foundry, that American companies not in a position to draw on foreign subsidiaries for production were in for trouble. American Machine & Foundry manufactures a wide variety of machinery, including bowling equipment; but White was speaking of many industries — machine tools, automobiles, sewing machines, office machinery. The competition of foreign imports could be met only if an American firm could draw on its own foreign plant for both components and finished products, the industrialist said.

Industry was doing more than talking, however; the trek

abroad was continuing. "Investing in West Europe seems to have become a new bandwagon for American industrialists," wrote the *Journal of Commerce* on March 10. "Few of the big companies have failed to climb aboard and accommodations will have to be managed for the many more certain to come."

The Old World had become the "new frontier," the newspaper went on, and few annual reports by U. S. companies did not make mention of some foreign manufacturing plans. According to estimates, American industry was investing in new plant in Western Europe about $500 million a month at an annual rate.

Actually what was happening went deeper than foreign investment; American companies — at least the larger ones — were going through a revolution in their point of view. The "Shape of the '60's" — a phrase currently much used by financial writers — was changing what advertising men like to call the "corporate image." Less and less were large companies thinking of themselves as American enterprises with foreign operations. More and more the idea of the international enterprise was taking hold, the "world company" in which domestic sales were but one segment of the world market, and where domestic production was simply a division of productive capacity spread perhaps half around the earth.

Such a company might be expected to carry on its research wherever it could do so most effectively and most cheaply, and to hold funds in whatever currency might be used most advantageously in the purchase of raw materials and other supplies. Top production management would be thinking in terms of where costs would be lowest, for the world as well as the domestic market. Sales executives would be judging where the maximum sales effort could be applied throughout the world with the greatest realizable return.

In January *Business Week* gave special attention to this

development, noting how certain companies had already readjusted their top management structure to conform to the realities of the new age. General Electric was one of several companies mentioned, a company which had been watching developments abroad for years.

Previously General Electric had operated abroad through its International General Electric Company Division, and in Canada through Canadian G. E. Now G. E. has created an International Group on a level with its Consumer Products Group, its Atomic, Electronic & Defense Products Group, and its Apparatus and Industrial Group. Each of these groups is headed by an executive who is a part of the top management team.

Another company cited was Smith-Corona, whose management structure was changed to allow "marketing strategy [that] will encompass the world. Some products, such as the lower priced portables, will be imported; other equipment will be made here and sold abroad. Additional facilities abroad will tap more third country markets."

In the *Harvard Business Review* there appeared late in 1959 an article by Gilbert H. Clee and Alfred di Scipio of McKinsey & Company, Inc., management consultants, which went deeper into the why and wherefore of the changes management was making in its approach to business overseas. In this piece, Clee and Di Scipio noted that Colgate-Palmolive had sales abroad ten years ago amounting to $86.9 million, as against a domestic gross of $203.9 million. But in 1958 the company did a foreign gross of $262 million, as against $271 million in domestic sales. The record of earnings is even more startling. Ten years ago foreign sales produced only a little over 16 per cent of profits; whereas earnings from foreign operations in 1958 were actually considerably larger than those derived from domestic sales. As another illustration, in the same year National Cash Register did almost half its gross volume outside the United States.

Such companies are being forced to readjust their outlook to new market patterns. Of great significance to them is the fact that profit margins are generally larger, and sales potentials greater, in foreign markets than in the United States.

This development, this new industrial internationalism, the emergence of the "world company," is but another expression of the natural economic forces which today press the free world toward greater economic unity. Just as the deficit in our balance of payments forces us to guard the integrity of the dollar in relation to other currencies, and forbids us the latitude in monetary policy that we had in the past, so does the world company dictate that wage levels in the United States must bear some relation to wage levels outside the United States. For years to come, concerns here will be able to pay higher cash wages than their competitors abroad, or than they themselves pay in their own foreign plants. But there is a limit to the differential, which contradicts the position of union leaders who assert that an ever-rising wage level is sound because it creates a greater purchasing power which in turn is needed to insure full production and prosperity.

An almost opposite point of view is today justified by the facts. An ever-increasing wage level will cost us markets, and hence production, and hence jobs, both in the world and the domestic markets. Already the differential between foreign and U. S. wages is too great in many industries; while on others we are perhaps just at the danger point, where if wages rise more rapidly than productivity in the future, we shall see a greatly accelerated migration of production, and jobs, overseas.

These world companies now coming into being reflect the realities of the new age. They have in a sense themselves reached across national economic boundaries. Without the need of tariff protection or the shield of quotas, and with a vested interest in sound currencies and free convertibility, they point the direction which the future economic organization of the free world will have to follow if we are not to revert to segmented economic nationalism, and to the protectionism which has written such tragic history in the past. To the extent that these companies can make their influence felt in political Washington, we shall be allowed to move toward a constructive foreign economic policy. To the extent that their influence is denied, or counterbalanced by other voices, we shall be in danger in the years ahead.

XXII

When Will Labor Speak?

As of this writing, labor has been strangely silent on most of the international economic issues facing the nation today. With a few exceptions, so have the politicians. But those industries wanting protection have not been so hesitant.

"Protectionist Rumblings Spread" ran the title of an article in *Business Week* in mid-March, and at about the same time the Tariff Commission appealed to a Congressional appropriations subcommittee for a 15 per cent budget increase needed to handle its heavy work load. In the last six months of 1959, a total of twenty-seven new cases was initiated, compared to thirty during all of 1959. "At this rate," said the Commission chairman, Joseph E. Talbot, "we shall double our work load during this year."

The imports of foreign goods were rising, and those industries affected were reacting as they found themselves touched on the always sensitive profit nerve.

The position of the administration has been to give no more ground than it had done already in the years since taking office. Ahead in September lay one of the most important meetings in years of GATT (the General Agreement on Tariffs and Trade), and the government did not want its representatives to arrive with their position weakened by what might seem to the rest of the world like a United States retreat toward the protectionist camp.

In Congress, however, there were protectionist bills pending. Senator Kenneth B. Keating of New York, for instance, was sponsoring a measure which would relate tariffs to wage rates. Aimed at "sweatshop labor," this law was a variation of the old "flexible tariff" idea which dates back to the 1920's, when Republicans sought some scientific formula for arriving at rates.

Broadly, the theory of flexible tariffs is that U. S. duties should rise against a foreign manufacturer who paid low wage rates, and drop as companies abroad raised their wages and improved working conditions. It was a noble if unrealistic theory, for it set up the ideal of using the rich American market as an incentive to lead other nations to "see the light" and follow in the "American way."

The idea was found unworkable, however. Not only was it impossible for tariff officials here to determine European costs, or for that matter what wage rates foreign plants were actually paying; the whole concept was obviously naïve. The wage rates of the world are set by various factors, in large part by competitive conditions in various domestic markets as well as the world markets; and only those bemused by the dream of sole American economic grandeur can conceive of European companies adjusting their wages just to be able to penetrate a market in the United States. Yet the broad idea still fascinates those who seek a painless method of allowing wage costs as between the United States and the rest of the industrial world to equalize. It is said that Walter Reuther has long sought some plan generally along this line.

Actually the Keating bill violates the essential principle of flexible tariff, for it is flexible only on the upside; and the measure can be considered protectionist. It is strongly supported by those both in labor and in industry who seek further protection of domestic markets against goods made overseas.

Meanwhile, a few protests about American foreign investment abroad — the trend toward the world company — were beginning to be heard.

As far back as April of 1959, Senator William Proxmire of Wisconsin proposed a Senate investigation of American firms setting up subsidiaries or branches abroad.

Said the Senator: "In at least two industries vital to employment in my state — machine tools and tractors — American companies have recently, in effect, transferred part of their production from Wisconsin to foreign countries . . . in the case of one company . . . the 40 per cent of production that used to go into export is now produced in a foreign factory with a loss of more than 2000 Wisconsin jobs . . .

"Reliable reports indicate that this export of American jobs has just begun. The combination of available American capital, American automation and know-how fused with low foreign wages is not only cutting a terrible swath in the export market for American factories, it is beginning to cost them their domestic markets . . ."

In the following November, John L. Lewis in an interview in *U. S. News & World Report* mentioned the subject, saying that there was "chaos coming in that field. It will be a political issue one of these days."

But Lewis's real blast was reserved for his retirement speech in January before 600 delegates of the United Mine Workers, the union he had so long led.

It was a dramatic occasion, and Lewis, pointing a battle-scarred finger, lashed out in his best manner.

"The flight of American capital . . . is a problem that will attract the attention of this nation in the years to come. Many of our manufacturers have items suitable for trade in the world marts but are finding it impossible to manufacture their goods in the United States under our standards of wages and living and collateral costs. So they are going abroad and are erecting production plants in foreign countries. One thousand American concerns already have plants that they erected in foreign countries. There they produce articles of trade which they had produced in their own American plants. There they produce articles with money earned under the American flag, under the free enterprise system. They are failing to reinvest under that same flag and under that same system. Many additional American concerns of magnitude in the commercial world are even now considering whether they are going to be forced to withdraw from the world markets or build production plants abroad, where there are low wages and standards of living conditions. There they can manufacture the same articles at less than they can do at home.

"You know, I used to know a baker in a fairly large town. His name was Heine and he only had one ad. He had it on the highway, a mile out of town, a highway that meets the four roads, and all it said was: 'Heine eats his own bread.' But, apparently American capital — in part — does not want to eat its own bread."

Why, as of this writing, has Lewis been the only labor leader to speak out on what is certainly a matter of profound concern to American workers?

A partial explanation may lie in the fact that it is a problem with which his union will not have to deal. Lewis has been protectionist when the domestic market for coal seemed threatened; for instance, he has always supported strongly a quota on imported oil. But American mines need neither protection against coal imports nor foreign production to keep them competitive.

Lewis himself is responsible for this. He has forced mechanization on the mines in this country ruthlessly, through wage demands which in the decade between 1948 and 1958 sent the daily pay of a miner from about $12 to

$26. Yet Appalachian bituminous sold in 1958 for just one cent a ton more than it sold for in 1948. Almost alone among world commodities it has not been affected by the inflation of the postwar years.

For this, Lewis's union paid a price, however, for as machines took over the work of men in the mines, employment in the industry fell from 400,000 in 1948 to 200,000 in 1958. This might be Lewis's answer to the problem of imports and the building abroad of American-owned plant. But it was an answer that no other union leader could make. Lewis's position was unique in that coal was an industry with very large room for mechanization, and because the decline in employment could be tolerated in a dirty and dangerous business that despite its high wages does not attract younger men.

Yet sooner or later, the leaders of American labor will have to speak out on this issue, which threatens to upset quite radically the balance of power at the bargaining table which has been tilted toward labor now for a good many years.

A management with production facilities in several countries will be better able to stand a strike. It will be less susceptible to pressure by the threat of a work stoppage which might damage its competitive position. Its hand will be still further strengthened by the possibility, always implicit even if not stated, that it can counter wage demands by cutting back operations in the United States and increasing output in foreign plant. Conceivably under certain circumstances and in certain industries, workers in foreign plant could be used, in effect, as "strikebreakers," by a company's importing foreign output for the U. S. market during a work stoppage in domestic plant.

These are very touchy subjects. Management is going out of its way not to mention them, and union leaders too are silent over a situation in which probably they have not as yet formulated a position. The whole question, actually, is a Pandora's box, which nobody wants to open; for once opened, the issues which will swarm out may well bring about a flame of industrial bitterness such as we have not seen since the rise in power of American labor during the New Deal.

Consider the position of James Carey of the International Union of Electrical Workers, AFL-CIO, the so-called IUE. Carey faces a continual challenge from the Independent United Electrical Workers, or UE, which was divorced from the AFL-CIO in 1949 amidst charges of Communist domination. Since that time the UE has come back to contest the IUE in many union elections. It has won a few, and lost others by the slimmest of majorities — 3444 to 3175, for instance, in an election of one of the industry's largest locals, that of the General Electric Company's plant at Lynn, Mass.

Now the electrical industry perhaps more than any other is not only building plant abroad, but importing parts made abroad for assembly here. Electrical workers read of Radio Corporation's plans for a large electronic network in southern Italy, for instance, or of Admiral's plant in Milan, or of Raytheon's in Palermo. These same workers are handling parts made in Japan in assembling transistor radios and much other equipment. Here is visible and tangible evidence of production jobs lost to the industry here.

How long before resentment at foreign plant and foreign component begins to mount among the rank and file of the locals? And how long, given the jurisdictional struggle between the IUE and UE, before Carey will be forced to take a stand against it?

These are uncomfortable questions, which hang over unions other than the electrical workers. At the moment we are trying to pretend that they don't exist. But they do exist, and they are likely to become one of the major political issues of the present decade. For as labor finds itself losing economic power at the bargaining table in the big industries, it will almost certainly turn to political action in order to readjust the balance in its favor — that is, to seek legislative or administrative restrictions on the import of components and investment in foreign plant.

To this it will be forced by its membership, even though its leaders may realize the danger of what would follow. For such restrictions would prevent American industry from remaining competitive. It would lose us markets abroad. It would also lose us segments of our domestic market, unless at the same time tariffs on finished products were erected to shut out imports. The great danger is just this, that the present migration of plant abroad may lead labor toward an outright protectionist position.

If you restrict foreign investment, foreign procurement of parts, you damage the competitive position of industries; and when you damage industry's ability to compete, you invite protection — in fact, protection becomes the logical next step.

In the last twenty-five years we have made great strides in freeing trade under the Reciprocal Trade Agreements Act. But it is worthwhile noting that we have been able to do this largely at the tolerance of several very powerful political voices. The United Auto Workers have favored free trade. There lay their own best interests; only within the last three years have we imported more cars than we exported from the assembly lines in Detroit. The steelworkers too have stood for liberal trade policies, again because the industry here was a net exporter of steel. But today imports crowd the big mills in light products like barbed wire, nails, reinforcing rods and, in some parts of the country, even in heavier shapes.

How long will these unions retain a position which both threatens their power at the bargaining table and may cost their membership jobs in the years ahead?

Of the four leading unions in the AFL-CIO, the Textile

Workers are already protectionist, and the electrical workers are very close to it. In fact, at the AFL-CIO meeting in
the fall of 1959, an effort was made by these unions to swing
the whole American labor movement toward the protectionist camp. The move was not successful, in part because labor
leaders on the whole have traditionally favored freer trade,
knowing as they do the traps of protectionism and understanding its role in leading us into the deep depressions of
the past.

But the time may be approaching when the spokesmen of
American unions will be forced by their own membership to
reverse this traditional position (as has already been the
case in the Textile Workers). Only in the imagination of
the public relations men of industry are labor leaders dark
schemers who lead the honest, God-fearing, job-loving
worker to those outrageous demands which keep corporate
officials awake through the long nights. In reality the shoe
is on the other foot, and the problem of top union leadership is to hold the rank and file of the locals down to reason-
able, or at least attainable, demands.

Back in the early 1930's it was industry which swung us
into the protectionism that culminated in the disaster of the
Hawley-Smoot Act. It is today not too difficult to see such a
disaster recurring, initiated this time by certain industries
and supported by American labor under the politically in-
flammatory slogan: "Stop the Exporting of American Jobs
Overseas."

XXIII

A North Atlantic Economic Community?

Over the Paris meetings in March hung the great questions:

How to avoid trade war between the two European blocs?

How to avoid the segmentation of the free world into blocs which, discriminating against each other, would dissipate prosperity and economic strength?

Meanwhile the Four Wise Men were working on a blueprint for a new North Atlantic organization to replace the old OEEC. This would be presented in mid-April at a meeting of the twenty nations who would hold membership, the Inner Six of the Common Market, the Outer Seven of Britain's Free Trade Area, five nations affiliated with neither bloc, and Canada and the United States.

This was the Dillon Plan, presented in Paris in January by the American Undersecretary of State. An era had ended, and another was opening. Europe had rebuilt, and in that rebuilding loosened forces which were pressing the free world toward economic unity. As distance shrank, trade and investment were rising, reaching across national frontiers.

C. Douglas Dillon, the banker turned diplomat and statesman, former ambassador to France, had understood what was happening and indicated the means with which the problem arising might be met. Under his plan the United States and Canada would, as a first step, join with the new Europe in an organization which would establish greater economic cooperation, and initiate joint efforts to aid the underdeveloped nations. Here was the joint challenge of an age which the Europeans had already named the "Dillon Era," in a tribute to the ability and farsightedness of this very remarkable young man.

Back in the United States, however, there was mounting economic restlessness as the competition of foreign imports cut deeper, while in Europe the rift between the Outer Seven and the Inner Six seemed to be widening. In a sense Dillon had on his hands a race with time.

The ideal organization of the free world economy would be a single North Atlantic Common Market, and perhaps eventually a single economic bloc of all free nations, including Japan. Such a bloc would abolish tariffs, quotas and other trade barriers. It would allow investment capital to flow freely. Its national currencies would be freely convertible. It might even eventually adopt a common currency, and a single central bank.

Of course, such an ideal would take years to realize. Trade barriers cannot be brought down overnight without distortions in national economies too painful to be tolerated. But the ideal, the ultimate objective, could be established, and the mechanism constructed with which to work. While this might be the task of a generation or two, the very fact that the end had been defined clearly would give nations a sense of economic purpose, which in itself would carry the task forward. Much of today's cynicism, the unwillingness of industry to think in terms other than its own profit and loss accounts, stems from the lack of any national objective. Industrialists can place the public good above their own immediate self-interest only when a national purpose has been agreed upon and clearly defined.

The logical time for the launching of this idea of a single North Atlantic bloc would have been between the close of the Korean War and 1955. By then European recovery was assured, and the outline of today's problems was beginning to appear. Those were the years of international good feeling, and of high prestige for the United States. We could then have led such a move toward the coalescing of national economies as the natural outgrowth of the Marshall Plan. Khrushchev had not at that time brought the Soviet Union out of the Marxist mystique into the modern world of trade and competition, and Europe still dreaded not only the power of the Soviet Union but the possible rise of communism among its own workers. Above all, then, the United States was still the sole economic giant. And the structure of such a grouping of nations certainly would have reflected our power and prestige. We could then have called the tune about as we wished.

But much of the good feeling of the mid-1950's has been dissipated — in the Suez crisis, as just one illustration, as far as the United States is concerned. European recovery has been swift. Nations have grown stronger and recaptured foreign markets lost in the war years. This means that vested interests in trade have been established. Europe is more competitive now, and the stakes are larger; therefore the sacrifices necessary for unity are greater. Antagonisms — particularly of Britain against Germany, and Britain against France — have appeared.

Thus the groundwork of a North Atlantic economic community is more difficult to lay today. We missed the golden opportunity of the mid-1950's, choosing to urge unity on Europe in the form of the Common Market, while holding ourselves aloof. Now the Common Market has come into being, and to hold ourselves aloof is no longer possible except at great peril. We must do now what we failed to do five years ago, take the initial steps toward a cooperation with Europe that ultimately could lead to some form of economic organization of the NATO powers.

This will be very difficult. Five years ago, it would not have been easy; but the problems then would have been largely economic and political attitudes on this side of the Atlantic. Now the problems are in part in Europe, while at the same time the difficulties here have greatly increased.

Ten years ago, American industry dominated the world market. It had little to fear from such competition as could be exerted by the still war-shattered industries of Europe and Japan. Foreign imports to this country were only a trickle, and the most often heard complaint of American corporations was not that they lacked sufficient protection, but that foreign nations were protecting their own industries by discrimination against American goods in markets overseas.

There was a good deal of justification for this complaint, for certainly the United States has not been the sole, or at times even the chief, offender in the use of barriers against trade. But Europe and Japan, faced with the task of rebuilding industries and plagued by shortages of foreign exchange, had no choice but to hold imports to an amount which could be financially and competitively digested during their period of recovery. And with certain exceptions it can be said that as their economies strengthened they progressively relaxed their barriers. They had to. They had to export, and to export they had to import, a fact understood in greater depth by foreign nations than as yet by the United States.

As foreign nations have tended to free trade, we in the United States, however, have tended to tighten it — or at least the demand, the political pressure, to tighten it has increased. Large segments of American industry today besiege Congress for tariffs and quotas, and seek through technical loopholes or escape clauses in the present laws to thwart the entrance of foreign goods to the markets of the United

States. This is a reflection of competition from a new and stronger Europe, and a new and stronger Japan. But it is a development that will make any economic drawing together of the nations of Europe with Canada and the United States much more difficult now than it would have been some years ago when the output of American factories had the final say in the markets of the world.

But in the rising tide of protectionism in the United States lies the seed of more than a possible failure to meet the central economic problem of our times, which is international economic organization. Here is a path to eventual economic disintegration of the sort that sooner or later in the past has led to political disintegration and often armed conflict.

Trade barriers, as they rise, strangle a nation in a process that works both ways. Domestic markets may be denied to foreign goods and thus pre-empted by domestic manufacturers. But in this process, broadly and over the long run, no one gains; for the loss of business by the exporting nation results in a lowering of economic activity which in its turn prevents the purchase abroad by that nation of goods it might otherwise have imported. The result is a drying up of output in both nations, and a tendency toward economic stagnation. Foreign trade is a great economic stimulant; its loss, a depressant of the most serious nature. This whole process is exaggerated by the foreign exchange difficulties which always follow an artificial restriction on commerce overseas. Furthermore, protectionism breeds retaliation, for trade is a two-way street; and when it is practiced by one country, others follow, and the result is a creeping paralysis that quickly reaches across economic frontiers.

There is one proposition that can be stated almost axiomatically: If the barriers against trade rise in this country, if American labor joins with strong enough segments of American industry to turn the United States away from the slow process of trade liberalization we followed between 1934 and 1949, then the clouds of depression will gather again just as they did thirty years ago. In that eventuality, the American people — believing that our domestic economy has become almost depression-proof, that the tragic experience of the 1930's "can never happen again" — will suffer one of the great disillusionments of the century.

XXIV

What the U. S. Has to Fear

Is PROTECTIONIST sentiment on the increase in the U. S.? In March the magazine *Business Week* looked over the scene and answered in effect, Yes, but that the issue was still in balance. "All the elements of a strong protectionist tide are in the making. But so are the forces of freer trade, the pushers of exports." The situation was "mushy," the magazine said, and would probably dawdle along until after the election in November.

On March 29, the *New York Daily News* started a series titled: "BARGAINS OR BOOMERANG? . . . Low-Cost Imports Imperil Us."

The newspaper admitted a dilemma.

On the one hand, it is generally acknowledged in government and in numerous industrial circles that a free flow of Free World goods into America has become an economic necessity and an important factor in our national security . . .

On the other hand, the torrent of low-priced foreign products pouring into the United States has already resulted in the destruction of long established industries and is threatening, here and abroad, to create unemployment, depression and even starvation in some areas.

The *News* was not very successful in pinpointing the "destruction of long established industries," nor the "unemployment, depression and even starvation in some areas."

The newspaper cited imports of foreign cars, up from 1500 to 261,000 in twelve years. Yet earnings of the industry in 1959 — despite the steel strike and consequent loss of the cream of the new-model market in the fall — stood at $1.6 billion, the second-best year on record, and double the earnings of 1958.

The textile industry, perennial wringer of its hands over imports, also received the sympathy of the *Daily News:* ". . . the economic situation [here] is especially acute. During the last three months of 1959, imported cotton in the form of bolts of cloth, shirts, blouses and other items of everyday wear rose at a colossal rate — setting an all-time record of a billion square yards."

Investment analysts following the textile industry seemed somewhat less alarmed over the situation of the mills, however.

"The textile industry was one of the bellwethers of the economy in 1959," said the Value Line, one of the best investment services, in mid-January. "Industry-wide sales expanded 16 per cent over the 1958 level, and approached the record high of 1951. Higher average selling prices have led to even more substantial earnings gain."

Coming down to cases, the *News* quoted former Army Secretary Robert T. Stevens (a casualty of the McCarthy hearings), who heads J. P. Stevens Company, one of the nation's largest textile producers. Stevens had recently called for drastic action by the U. S. government, "unless it considers the textile industry to be expendable." And the newspaper went on to call attention to a recent full-page newspaper advertisement that Stevens' company had run:

It is a known fact that increasing imports of yard goods and garments have seriously hurt the textile industry. In a period of continued prosperity, many mills have closed their doors — with the resultant loss of American jobs.

The J. P. Stevens Company itself had not been hurt, however. Net earnings had risen from $2.60 a share in 1958 to $4.51 in 1959, the highest level in eight years. Nor did the Value Line fear much for the company's future.

"J. P. Stevens is participating handsomely in the current rise in textile industry sales and earnings," the service wrote in January in recommending the purchase of the stock to its clients. Under an assumed rise in gross national product for the country over the next few years, the Value Line projected an increase in sales for the company from $459 million in 1959 to $610 million in 1962-64 . . . and saw an increase in the dividend rate.

Actually while continually asking for tariffs and quotas the industry has in recent years sold more textiles abroad than were imported into the United States.

Among other voices raised in the cause of protection even while the meetings in Paris were going on, were Smith-Corona and Royal McBee, which joined in asking the Tariff Commission for a 30 per cent duty on imported typewriters. This was an odd request, to put it mildly; for both companies have built plant abroad in which to manufacture not only for the world and European markets but also for the domestic market in the United States. Smith-Corona, as a matter of fact, had been cited earlier in the year by *Business Week* as an example of the new concept of a world company. (See page 150.) E. E. Mean, executive vice-president, was quoted as saying, "The important thing is, we are a world company."

A world company needing tariffs? The importers of European typewriters, in opposing the request of the two American companies for a duty, pointed out that of the 450,000 machines imported to the United States during the previous year, about one-third had been made abroad in foreign plant owned by American firms.

Many of the chemical companies too were in this position

of wanting the all-this-and-heaven-too of protection at home
with access to rapidly expanding markets overseas. Monsanto, for instance, had been one of the leaders in the industry in foreign investment; between 1953 and 1959 some $118
million went into its operations abroad. The company does
not publish a breakdown as between foreign and domestic
sales, but analysts estimated that in 1958 foreign sales
amounted to about $100 million, of which some $40 million represented exports from the United States.

Yet Monsanto chairman Edgar M. Queeny, retiring in
March, vigorously attacked the administration in what read
like a twin blast against foreign aid and liberalized trade,
saying that the United States had become the "world's milch
cow."

On the other side of the issue, the voices were less strident.
These were of the big exporting industries, and of many
companies which understood well the danger of tightening
trade barriers at any time and particularly at a crucial moment like the present.

The big steel companies, drawing much of their ore from
abroad, were not buying a protectionist policy, even though
steel imports were increasing. Neither was the automobile
industry, although here too the export-import balance had
turned unfavorable in recent years. The inconsistency of
advocating protection in the United States while maintaining foreign plant manufacturing for both the domestic and
world markets was apparently quite evident to Detroit.

Furthermore, there were always the brave voices — the
men who stood for freer trade as a matter of principle even
though they themselves were engaged in an industry in
which imports could hurt.

For years Charles H. Percy of Bell & Howell in Chicago
has stumped the country urging freer trade. Yet the company's products — cameras and sound projectors — were of
the sort in which foreign competition might well be serious.

This is an industry in which the tariffs have been brought down sharply. Yet Bell & Howell has been able to maintain its markets, both here and abroad. It has done this by the efficiency of its domestic operations — between 1943 and 1955, output per worker was increased by ninety times — and by a competitive policy of buying parts wherever they can be had at the best price. An official of the company explains it thus: ". . . our various manufacturing divisions know that at any time we can secure components of equal quality more economically from domestic or foreign suppliers abroad, we will do so. This makes each division of the company competitive . . ."

Bell & Howell's record speaks for itself. In an industry where wage costs represent a very large percentage of total costs, and which is particularly susceptible to foreign competition, gross has risen from $16.9 million in 1950 to an estimated $63 million in 1959.

Said Percy at a Congressional hearing a few years back: "We have used the threat of foreign competition with our own manufacturing executives and design engineers to ask them to develop designs that are ingenious, to have them develop tools that will back up the American worker, employing his abilities in the way an American worker earning over two dollars an hour has to be employed . . ."

Asked by Senator Flanders of Vermont if his company was dependent on tariff protection, Percy replied simply: "If we were, sir, I would sell my stock in the company."

Actually Bell & Howell buys few parts abroad, and during the period in which it has been employing its policy of competitive buying of components, its employment rose from 900 to 4000. There were no jobs lost here.

Behind the division of industries, and companies within industries, on this issue of protectionism, there were two other factors noticeable in the opening months of the current year. One of these was a kind of grass-roots surge of

economic isolationism. The other was that whereas tariffs
had formerly been favored as a means of protection, quotas
were now being demanded.

Both developments are serious. Quotas which limit the
physical volume of goods that can be brought in throw up a
higher wall than is possible with any but the most unreason-
able duty. The sort of thing that recently exploded into the
"Buy American" move in certain Midwestern cities — stick-
ers on merchandise, a publicized hullabaloo urging the buying of American products in order to "back" America and
protect American jobs — reflects an emotionalism which has
no place in the logically balanced world of economics in
which we live today.

It may be argued that tariffs are necessary as a means to
orderly transition, that they should be used, for instance,
as a way of easing the emergence of the United States from
its historic economic isolation into the reality of the world
that has evolved in recent years. (This has been denied by
some economists, notably the late Sumner H. Slichter of
Harvard, who believed that we should abolish all duties immediately, even if we did so unilaterally.) Used in this
manner, tariffs can be progressively reduced as the adjustment is made.

Certainly nothing can be said for raising tariffs, however,
or for refusing to reduce them whenever possible; for the
effect of this is to subsidize inefficiency at the expense of the
consumer and to breed the sort of stagnation which spells
industrial death.

Who would deny that the penetration of the European car
into the American market has benefited not only the American people, but the industry itself as well? It was the little
Volkswagen, the Dauphine and the smartly designed and
well-made British cars that awakened Detroit from its night-
mare of towering fins and ever-heavier incrustation of
chrome. The designers and engineers of an industry which

had always been especially our own were caught napping. The European imports have given us the new compact models from Detroit.

The same is true of the sewing machine and the typewriters and office machinery industries. It is interesting that when the dying Underwood Corporation was bought by the Italian firm of Olivetti — one of the best-run companies in Europe — Olivetti canceled orders that Underwood had taken in certain kinds of equipment. The new Italian management did not consider this equipment good enough to be sold under the Olivetti name.

Foreign competition is in fact vitalizing, just as is domestic competition. It breeds resourcefulness, new techniques, new designs, new ideas. American industry has always given at least strong lip service to competition as the prime ingredient of our free enterprise system. But competition today, if it is to mean anything, cannot be limited to national frontiers.

To anyone aware of what was happening in Europe in the early months of 1960, the shape of events in the United States was such as to cause a good deal of concern. The mutterings for protection were mounting. There was the great question mark of labor's position. There seemed to be, just beneath the service, a growing and almost calculated insensitivity to the realities of the new decade.

Meanwhile the various political candidates, rushing around to the popularity contests of state primaries, were pumping hands and smiling on all who would smile back at them. If they were aware of the great issues hanging over the world, they did not betray this knowledge in the speeches being written for them by hired speech writers. The American voter was being promised everything — the farmer more protection against a free market, despite the billions already tied up in crop surpluses; older people, free medical, hospital and nursing care.

The pollsters were measuring the popularity of the candidates, and the candidates were quoting the pollsters, and the political writers were covering it all as sports writers cover a world series baseball game.

In Europe, the March meetings which had searched for a way to avoid a split between the Inner Six and the Outer Seven adjourned without settling anything, the issue left on ice at least until July. Nikita Khrushchev visited Paris, and Harold Macmillan visited Washington. And, commenting on the two visits, Volney D. Hurd of the *Christian Science Monitor* wrote: "A whole new power shift may be in the making . . ."

Khrushchev was trying to break the Paris-Bonn axis, core of the Inner Six. Macmillan was trying to convince Washington that continued support by the United States of the Inner Six as against the Outer Seven could only endanger the political and economic status of the whole free world.

The tenseness of the situation was revealed in an editorial in the London *Times* on a remark said to have been made by the British Prime Minister to Secretary of State Herter:

Macmillan is said to have recalled "in a scholarly manner" that it was Britain's historic role to crush Napoleonic ambitions to integrate Europe and that should France and Germany go on the road towards a unified Western Europe, Britain, in the long run, had no other choice but to lead another peripheral alliance against them. He added that in the time of Napoleon, Britain allied itself with Russia to break the French Emperor's ambitions.

Later the British Foreign Office minimized the implied warning in the allusion to Russia, saying that the Prime Minister had only been citing a historical fact. But by then the message had been put across. Britain, in the forces swirling around the two trade blocs in Europe, was playing for keeps.

Who knows how much the rising tide of protectionism in

the United States was aggravating the situation in Europe? American trade policy is watched closely by economic ministers of foreign nations. Ahead lay the most important negotiations on economic matters in years: the major GATT meeting in September, when new tariff levels were to be thrashed out, and the further efforts to bridge the gap between the Outer Seven and the Inner Six. What would be the position of the United States in these conferences? Would its emissaries to GATT be hamstrung by political pressures at home that would prevent further trade liberalization? The American Undersecretary of State had proposed a new economic organization of the 20 North Atlantic and European nations to succeed OEEC and draw the free world closer together. But was a drift toward economic isolationism in the United States to emasculate this proposal, reducing it to a meaningless expression of good intentions, by tying Dillon's hands?

If this was to be the case, Europe would have to follow a different policy than in the past, for the central truth of the economic world today is that no unity, or real organization even of Europe, is possible without the active participation of the United States. The industrial strength of America, its wealth and productiveness, its lands, its factories, its monetary gold stocks are such that it cannot remain outside the economic community of Europe without the erection of artificial barriers which would smother both Europe and the United States in the end.

The truth of this is established, in fact, by the way in which we have in a sense come a full turn in our reaction to the formation, first of the Common Market and then of the Free Trade Area. We had supported the Common Market. Then when it had come into being, we had seen a danger in its merging with the Free Trade Area into an economically solidified Europe that would in a few years have developed economic power to match even our own. But now we feared the opposite, the splitting of Europe into blocs which would discriminate not only against each other, but against us. This is not as paradoxical as it sounds. We have only one thing to fear, and that is any organization of Europe that *does not* include the United States.

No one understands this central fact better than the British, who must think in world terms because of their dominions. Britain protested strongly a proposed speed-up in putting into effect the provisions of the Common Market — and is actually opposed to the Common Market — largely out of a fear of a Germany rising in political and economic strength. But such fears would not exist in an Atlantic economic community of the sort that might eventuate out of the Dillon proposal, and which would include Canada and the United States. In the larger, inclusive group, no one could dominate the continent of Europe, for the doors would be opened for all to trade.

On the other hand, if the United States is turning back to economic isolationism, then to British eyes there are only the blocs — one eventually to be led by Germany, and one by themselves. And if there are to be only blocs, then the main concern of the British must be the well-being of the one they will lead.

In short, the day has passed when the United States can cooperate in European unity by sitting back with a checkbook in its hands, uttering pious words of good advice. The checkbook is no longer needed, the advice has been taken. Now the United States has to play in the game, or withdraw. If it plays, the cause of economic unity of the West can be won and the free world organized economically. If it does not play, there is only the old power game that has been played for centuries, played now, however, in economic rather than political terms.

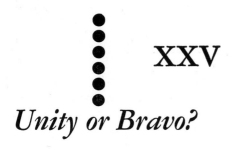

XXV

Unity or Bravo?

THE INDUSTRIAL NATIONS of the free world today face two dangers, one internal, the other from without. The internal danger is that economic rivalries may set them warring amongst themselves economically. This would almost certainly bring about conditions which would send us once more into a serious deflationary spiral, a depression of sufficient depth to threaten our whole economic way of life.

The danger from without — in which the Soviet Union plays a role as yet not precisely determined — lies in the underdeveloped areas of the world, and particularly in China. Here is the great issue, the great challenge, the problem which, if it is to be solved, will occupy the best minds of the generation now taking over the reins of both industry and government. Here is the fire to test the will and the imagination of democracy and capitalism. Here is our ultimate test.

Africa and Latin America are seething. Political instability is reflecting the economic aspirations of millions who are demanding an end to poverty, and who see in industrialization the only possible means to that end. But industrialization is not easy of accomplishment, and can be brought about today only by paying a high price either in time or in freedom.

Industrialization can be had relatively quickly, as with the Soviet Union and Japan, but only if the living standards of a people can be kept down ruthlessly in order to generate the capital needed — that is, out of the excess of production over consumption. Or it can be done more slowly, with higher living standards; and this means quite slowly, with the huge amounts of capital required to finance the industrial complex today. Thus speed can be bought only if a people are willing to submit to the impositions of low living standards, as were the people of the Soviet Union and Japan. This is hardly possible in Latin America or Africa.

The process can, of course, be speeded up by borrowing capital . . . either from governments or private sources. But the former is possible only to the degree that the people of already industrialized nations are willing to be taxed to provide the funds to lend — or to give in grants; while the latter presupposes a willingness of the borrower to allow the lender a fairly high return on his money, and sufficient political stability to assure him of getting his money back. Thus the question: how much will the people of Europe, the United States and even Japan allow themselves to be taxed in order to aid the development of the underdeveloped areas? And the second question: how many others in Latin America, Africa and Asia will follow in the Castro and Nasser path?

Then there is the special problem of China, on fire with a new Marxist ideology, seething with new vitality, the awakening giant with already roughly one-fourth of the population of the earth. Latin America and Africa could be plunged into economic and social chaos, which would be serious enough. But Red China, which is reported ready soon to explode its first nuclear weapon, can send the world roaring up in a pillar of fire.

These are dangers impossible to exaggerate, problems which unless solved could turn the course of history into another era of disruption such as followed the fall of classic civilization. And it is essential now, as we approach them, that we marshal the full strength and resourcefulness of the West. This we will not be able to do without economic organization. This we cannot do if we remain segmented, or coalesce into the supranationalism of blocs warring against each other in the realm of trade. And this we most certainly will be unable to do if we turn to the nationalistic protectionism which, experience should have taught us, leads to the sort of serious depression we have known in the past.

Actually if natural forces are not thwarted or distorted, they will carry us toward just this integrated organization that we need in order to meet the major issues of our times. The great divisive factor is the differential in living standards between Japan, Europe and the United States. But today industrial growth is more rapid in Japan than in Europe, and in Europe more rapid than in the United States. High prosperity means tight labor, and tight labor means rising wages — and wage costs, as distinct from wages — as the job-hungry worker is more productive than one who if he loses his job can get another by walking across the street (something being quite dramatically illustrated by the drop of output per man-hour in the tight labor market in West Germany today).

Thus today both cash wages and wage costs are rising faster abroad than they are here. This is not to say that the wage rates of the European or Japanese worker will rise to equal that of a worker in the United States. This will not come about for years, if ever. But many factors other than per-hour earnings go into labor costs; and it is costs which count, competitively. Actually, cash wages in Europe do not have to rise as much as might be imagined for industry in most lines in this country to be able to meet on equal grounds cost-wise with the output of European plant. When that happens, we could be close to the realization of the ideal of free trade.

The dangers, of course, lie in attempting to thwart the

natural forces that tend to bring us toward this equaliza-
tion: one danger is the temptation to raise trade barriers in
an effort to "protect" certain industries which become un-
economic in particular areas; another, equally serious,
would be an unwillingness to accept the fact that Japan and
Europe will show more economic growth than we in the
next twenty years. This danger is very real, for economic
growth has become almost a fetish to politicians, and to
many of the rest of us a source of national satisfaction and
pride.

However, it is neither possible nor desirable that our
national product in the United States show a rate of growth
equal to that of the two other free industrial areas. It is not
desirable because it would continue the present per-capita-
income differentials which prevent unity. And it is not possible because man's needs and wants are not infinitely
expandable. There comes a limit to per capita consumption
of food, to the number of cars and appliances per family, to
the clothes that people will buy. In rich high-income areas,
the year-to-year percentage of growth always tends to slow
down to some degree.

In this country economic expansion will be more and
more a reflection of the population increase. In Europe and
Japan it will reflect this factor, plus another — the rise in
living standards to a level more closely approaching ours.

The danger in not realizing this is that we may be turned
to political action designed to stimulate growth artificially:
cheap money, for instance, or huge government outlay re-
sulting in unbalanced budgets. Such a policy would in the
end not stimulate growth, but thwart it. While it might
allow the illusion of growth for a while, the net result would
be a boom-and-bust pattern. It would breed inflation here
in a world dedicated today to sound money. It would
weaken the position of the dollar as a reserve currency. It
would demonstrate that we were unable to learn to live

without inflation, a lesson which every nation will have to learn in the coming decade.

The American people have come a long way in recent years. The chance of a recurrence of the desperate depressions of the past is remote, unless we bring it upon ourselves by some economic folly. Security for most of us has been built into our economic structure. Never have opportunities been as wide. A large supply of consumer goods has given us ease and leisure. Industry is growing with solid momentum. Poverty — at least as we have known it in the past — has been all but erased.

Now we have reached a point in our economic history when we must, to a certain degree, settle for our past accomplishments for a while — or at least realize that national income is not a tree that can be force fed to reach the sky. Is that too much to ask of a mature and responsible people? Too high a price to pay for what could be a new era of peace and prosperity for Western man?

The alternative answers the question. Economic unity can lead over the years to political unity. Economic nationalism leads to isolationism and economic warfare, and as the barriers go up, so do the appropriations for weapons. To be isolated, you must be armed. Nations warring economically have in the past resorted to military action to protect or further their interests, and — the nuclear horror notwithstanding — they may do so again.

A generation hence we could have an economic NATO, a free world organized both economically and politically in which the huge amounts of capital now poured into armaments would be employed in developing the underdeveloped areas of earth. Or we could see a world quite different, in which the central fact would be not trade and investment but the warheads of waiting missiles . . . missiles under the sea in submarines where they cannot be detected, missiles buried in hidden pits sprinkled across the land.

Into the warheads of these missiles has been built a new lethalness of late. It is said now that the latest nuclear device is on the order of twenty megatons. That means that each of these bombs holds an explosive force equal to twenty million tons of TNT, which is about seven times the total amount of explosives used by all belligerents during the five years of World War II. This latest bomb is said to explode in a pillar of fire four miles in breadth. As it rises it sucks up hundreds of tons of matter which is then sprayed back upon the earth over an area of 1000 square miles in radioactive particles.

This instrument of what the military now term "overkill" is reported to carry the odd name of Bravo.

Organization of some kind we will have. We can have with small sacrifice an organization of reason. Or we can find ourselves organized by a balance of power imposed by the Bravo. That is the choice.